Ancient African Kingdoms

From the Kingdom of Kush to the Mali Empire,
Discover the History of Classical African
Civilizations

Jim Barrow

Table of Contents

7

Chapter One

LIST OF KINGDOMS IN PRECOLONIAL AFRICA

According to Vansina (1962), the five categories in which the sub-Saharan kingdoms in Africa (that is, Central Africa, South Africa, East Africa, and West Africa) were classified is given as follows:

- **Despotic Kingdoms**: These are kingdoms in which the rulers directly control both internal as well as external matters. Some of the kingdoms in this category include Ankole, the Kingdom of Kongo, and Rwanda.

- **Regal Kingdoms**: In regal kingdoms, the ruler is only responsible for handling external matters while the internal matters of the kingdom are handled by overseers. Usually, the chiefs and the king are a part of the same group and have the same religious beliefs.

- **Incorporative Kingdoms**: In these kingdoms, the ruler only handles matters that are external to the kingdom. He does not possess a lasting administrative connection to the chiefs, who are responsible for governing the provinces under the kingdom. Even after conquests, the regions governed by the chiefs of those provinces were not tampered with. Examples of such kingdoms are the Lunda and Luba Empires.

- **Aristocratic Kingdoms**: The paying of tribute was the only connection that the ruler of these kingdoms had with the provinces under them. Based on morphology, these kingdoms lie between regal kingdoms and federations.

- **Federations**: In these kingdoms, the matters that are external are handled by a council of elders, which is led by the ruler. An example of these kingdoms is the Ashanti Empire.

The kingdoms on this list are kingdoms that existed before the colonial periods in Africa. They fall into time periods in history referred to as "ancient," "post-classical," and "modern." Ancient history talks about the period when records of events in writing began, which is from 3600 BCE, more or less. Ancient history ended around 500 CE, in which period many great empires fell, including the Western Roman Empire in the Mediterranean, the Gupta Empire in India, and the Han Dynasty in China.

The post-classical era is the era between 500 CE to 1500 BCE in which events like the travels of Christopher Columbus and the conquest of Constantinople by the Ottoman Empire occurred. While modern history is the period where a more global network was created in the world, that is, when Europeans came in contact with Americans.

Precolonial Kingdoms of North Africa

Egyptian Empire

The Egyptian Empire, also called the New Kingdom, has been in existence for many years; however, the period between the 16th and 11th century BCE was the period when the kingdom enjoyed more prosperity throughout its existence. During the Second Intermediate Period (17th century), Kushites kept attacking the New Kingdom, and so in response, it expanded its territories into Nubia as well as the Near East.

After the death of Rameses III, three of his sons went on to become Pharaoh as Rameses IV, Rameses VI, and Rameses VIII. The kingdom suffered under droughts, flooding of the Nile, famine, civil unrest, and corrupt officers.

Kingdom of Kerma

Kerma kingdom was a kingdom in Kerma, Sudan. The kingdom flourished between 2500 and 1500 BCE, being the dominant kingdom in the region of Nubia from 2450 to 1450 BCE. The kingdom was established in Upper Nubia, currently occupied by modern-day northern and central Sudan; afterward, the kingdom's territory extended to Lower Nubia and to the Egyptian border. The kingdom stood against Egypt between 1700 and 1500 BCE; around 1500 BCE, it was incorporated into the New Kingdom (Kingdom of Egypt).

Carthaginian Empire

The Carthaginian Empire was a powerful empire that exercised dominance over the western Mediterranean until the middle of the 3rd century BCE. The capital of the empire was called Carthage, founded in 814 BCE. The empire was a cosmopolitan one, and it engaged Rome in a lot of battles called the Punic Wars between 264 and 146 BCE, threatening its power; it was in 146 BCE that Rome finally defeated the empire and forced all the states in Phoenicia under the empire to abide by Roman rule.

Kingdom of Blemmyes

The Blemmyes are people who Greeks, Romans, and Egyptians believed to have emerged from the Eastern Desert. These people occupied Lower Nubia in the latter part of the 4th century, and there, they founded a kingdom. The kingdom had a lot of important cities whose walls were made of combined Egyptian, Hellenic, Roman, and Nubian components – these cities include Faras, Ballama, and Aniba. Although sources say that the kingdom was not centralized; instead, the tribal cities came together in a kind of hierarchy. After the rulers, the next officials in the hierarchy were the phylarchs (chiefs).

Ptolemaic Kingdom

The Ptolemaic Kingdom was a Hellenic state founded in Egypt in ancient times. This kingdom was established in 350 BCE by a companion of Alexander the Great, Ptolemy I Soter. The kingdom existed up until 30 BCE, when Cleopatra passed away. The kingdom extended from eastern Libya to the Sinai and south to Nubia. The rulers of the kingdom took on the title of Pharaoh and asked artisans to portray their images on monuments in the styles and dresses of Egyptians so as to be accepted by Egyptian natives. The kingdom started waning due to strife between dynasties and foreign wars, which led it to rely heavily on the Roman Republic.

Kingdom of Kush

Kush was an antediluvian kingdom in the region of Nubia. The kingdom was founded along the Valley of the Nile, an area where modern-day northern Sudan and southern Egypt occupy. Egyptians identified the Kerma people as "Kush," and for many centuries, both Egypt and Kush engaged each other in sporadic trade, cultural exchange, and warfare. Many kingdoms in the Nubian region fell under the rule of the Kingdom of Egypt (1550 BCE to 1070 BCE); even though the Kushites built up a connection with the New Kingdom and they even had intermarriages, their culture was still different. During the time of the Late Bronze Age collapse, the Kush people went on to establish another kingdom in Napata, an area which is present-day Karima, Sudan.

Kingdom of Numidia

The Kingdom of Numidia was an antediluvian kingdom that was located in present-day Algeria, and its territories also spanned to touch a part of Tunisia as well as Libya in the Maghreb. In the beginning, the kingdom was split into two tribes; these tribes were the Massylii, which was in the east, and the Masaesyli in the west. However, King Masinissa of the Massyli overcame Syphax of the Masaesyli during the Punic Wars (218 BCE to 201 BCE) and united Numidia into a single kingdom. To the west, the kingdom shared a border with the Kingdom of Mauretania, to the east with the Moulouya River, Africa Proconsularis (currently a part of Tunisia), to the north with the Mediterranean Sea, and to the south with the Sahara. Numidia is seen to be one of the first significant kingdoms in the Berber world and Algeria's history. This great kingdom met its end as a result of the civil war that existed between Caesar and Pompey in 46 BCE.

Kingdom of Makuria

Makuria is another kingdom in the region of Nubia; it was located in modern-day northern Sudan and southern Egypt. In the first instance, the kingdom spanned over the region of the River Nile, beginning from the Third Cataract down to the south of Abu Hamad, and even down to northern Kordofan. The name of the kingdom's capital was Dongola. The culture of this kingdom developed more between the 9th and 11th century; in the 13th and 14th century, however, the kingdom waned due to several reasons such as increased Egyptian hostility, internal discord, Bedouin invasions, and the shifting of trade routes such that the empire was reduced to rubble, losing most of its territories in the south.

Kingdom of Nobatia

Nobatia or Nobadia is an ancient kingdom that was in Lower Nubia. Nobatia, Makuria, and Alodia combined to succeed the kingdom of Kush. The kingdom was founded in c. 400 and its territory was extended through the conquest of Blemmyes in the north; the kingdom then annexed the Blemmyes lands between the Second and Third Nile Cataract in the south. The kingdom adopted Coptic Christianity in c. 543, and by the 7th century, it was annexed into Makuria.

Kingdom of the Vandals and Alans

The Vandal kingdom is also known as the Kingdom of the Vandals and Alans; it was founded by the people of the Germanic Vandal. The period of the kingdom's predominance in North Africa and the Mediterranean is between c. 435 to c. 534. In the year c. 429, the Vandal peoples traveled over the ocean to North Africa from Hispania, and heading east on their journey, they subjugated the regions of present-day Morocco, Algeria, and Tunisia. The kingdom further overcame Carthage and the islands of Sicily, Sardinia, Corsica, and Mallorca, which were under Roman rule, challenging Roman authority, and the Romans retaliated by launching hostile expeditions unto the kingdom, which failed. In 534, Belisarius defeated the kingdom in the Vandalic War and annexed it into the Eastern Roman Empire, also referred to as the Byzantine Empire.

Kingdom of Nekor

The kingdom of Nekor was a domain that was located in modern-day Morocco, precisely the Rif region, and, the emirate was established in the year c. 710. The capital of the emirate was originally set at Temsaman before it was later moved to Nekor. The kingdom was subjugated under a group of Vikings in the year 859; these Vikings defeated the Moors' army in Nekor that tried to disturb their plunder in the region. The Vikings departed Morocco after eight days and headed for Spain.

Fatimid Caliphate

The Fatimid Caliphate was a caliphate of the 10th to 12th century CE; it covered a huge area of land in North Africa, beginning at the Red Sea, which was toward the east and to the west toward the Atlantic Ocean. The heart of the caliphate was Egypt, and the other regions that were part of the caliphate were Sudan, Sicily, the Levant, Maghreb, and the Hijaz. In the year 921, the Fatimid people moved their capital to Mahdia, a city of Tunisia.

Spanning from the late 11th century through to the 15th century, the caliphate dwindled ever so swiftly; with the coming of the year 1171, the territory of the caliphate was invaded by Saladin, who annexed it into the Abbasid Caliphate.

Almohad Caliphate

Almohad Caliphate was a Muslim kingdom of the Berbers in North Africa that was established during the 12th century. At the pinnacle of the empire's existence, much of the Iberian Peninsula and the Maghreb in North Africa were under its control. The empire continued to exercise authority over Iberia until Christian princes of Castile, Aragon, and Navarre formed an alliance in order to defeat Muhammad III "al-Nasir," who was overcome in Sierra Morena during the Battle of Las Navas de Tolosa (1199 to 1214).

Territories belonging to the Moors were lost after that battle, including Cordova and Seville. Soon after, the caliphate began to lose its territories bit by bit as various tribes and districts started revolting, thus enabling the Marinids (Banu Marin), who were the most effective of their enemies.

Mamluk Sultanate

The Mamluk Sultanate was an empire that made itself into a caliphate; it had land covering Egypt, the Levant, and Hejaz. The empire lasted from the period where the Ayyubid dynasty was overthrown through to the conquest of Egypt by the Ottomans in 1517. The rule of Mamluk is broken down into two periods: the first is referred to as the "Turkic" period, while the second is the "Circassian" period. The pinnacle of the empire's existence was during the Turkic rule, but the Circassian period came with a stage of its decline. A contributory factor to this decline was the reduction in revenues to the Mamluk-Venetian monopoly on the trans-Mediterranean trade caused by the expansion of the Portuguese empire into Africa and Asia.

Kingdom of Tlemcen

The kingdom of Tlemcen was a kingdom in the northwestern part of present-day Algeria; the kingdom's area of land spanned through Tlemcen to the Chelif bend and Algiers. The kingdom further stretched to the Moulouya River to the west, to the south, it reached the Sijilmasa and down east, to the Soummam River. A lack of geographical unity, internal disputes, a lack of fixed frontiers, and dependence on the Arabs for military troops were some of the reasons that led to the fall of the kingdom.

Marinid Sultanate

The Marinid Sultanate was a kingdom that existed between the 13th century to the 15th century that ruled over modern-day Morocco as well as other areas like Algeria and Tunisia in North Africa and southern Spain and Gibraltar. The empire's name was derived from a Zenata tribe of the Berbers known as Banu Marin. A sequence of the rapid takeover of rulership by each Sultan beginning in the year 1358, a division of the empire, and political anarchy were the series of events that set the stage leading to the complete destruction of the empire.

Republic of Salé

The Republic of Salé was a city-state that was established along the Bou Regreg river at Salé; it was a kingdom that was established in the 17th century by Moriscos from a town known as Hornachos in the western part of Spain. Moriscos were people of Muslim descent who were Christian converts by title and were victims of the mass deportation at the time of the Spanish Inquisition. The city is now a part of the kingdom of Morocco.

Precolonial Kingdoms of East Africa

Kingdom of Punt

The kingdom of Punt was an antediluvian kingdom that produced gold, aromatic resins, blackwood, ebony, ivory, and wild animals; the kingdom traded with the ancient kingdom of Egypt. The kingdom had lands that stretched through the Horn of Africa to southern Arabia; believed to be located toward the southeast of Egypt and covering littoral of present-day northeast Ethiopia, Djibouti, Somalia, Eritrea, the Red Sea, and Sudan.

Kingdom of Begwena

The kingdom of Begwena was a kingdom of North Africa in the early part of the Middle Ages with what is now northern Ethiopia as the heart of its empire; back then, the center of the kingdom was called Lalibela. The kingdom controlled land that stretched up to nearly 800 miles.

Kingdom of D'mt

D'mt was an empire that was located in Eritrea and the Tigray Region (northern Ethiopia). It was in existence between the 10th century and 5th century

BCE. However, not much is known about the kingdom as there are only a few surviving inscriptions and scant archeological work has been undertaken.

Harla Kingdom

This was a kingdom that existed in the 6th century that had what is now eastern Ethiopia as the heart of its empire. It traded with both the Ayyubid and Tang dynasties; it had land spanning between just over 500 yards east to west and almost 1,000 yards north to south. One study of the ancient kingdom shows that the people used knives; thus, their culture was common with that of the Islamic world of Arabia, Mesopotamia, the Levant, and Iberia.

Kingdom of Bazin

Bazin was an ancient kingdom of the medieval period with the heart of its empire in East Africa. The kingdom was among the six states in existence in the 9th century. The lands of the kingdom were based in between Aswan and Massawa.

Kingdom of Semien

Semien was an ancient kingdom that was also referred to as the Kingdom of Beta Israel; the heart of the kingdom was located in the northwestern part of the Ethiopian Empire. The kingdom ended in the year 1627 under the rule of Susenyos I after it engaged the Ethiopian empire in war and was conquered.

Kingdom of Kitara | Chwezi

The Kitara Empire, also called the Chwezi Empire, is the kingdom of the Bakitara people, which had dominance over territories stretching through the valley of the Nile and beyond. After the kingdom of Aksum broke into Makuria, Zagwe, Shewa, and Damot kingdoms in East Africa, a kingdom that broke into the south was the Kitara Empire. After a prophecy of the empire's demise came, many believed it; after an invasion into the empire, its people dispersed into Rwanda, Burundi, Ankole, and Eastern Congo.

Kilwa Sultanate

The Kilwa Sultanate was an ancient empire in medieval times that had Kilwa – an island outside modern-day Tanzania – as the heart of the empire. The empire is said to have been established by a Persian prince of Shiraz by the name of Ali ibn al-Hassan Shirazi. The kingdom went into decline when the Portuguese began to interfere with its rule beginning in the year 1500.

Kingdom of Medri Bahri

The kingdom of Medri Bahri was an antediluvian kingdom that occupied modern-day Eritrea that existed from the 12th century to the time it was taken over by Ethiopians. Once an independent kingdom, Medri Bahri was made to pay tributes to the Ethiopian Empire until the Ethiopian empire finally incorporated it into its kingdom.

Ethiopian Empire

Abyssinia, or as it is more popularly known, the Ethiopian Empire, was an empire that covered the territory of what is now Ethiopia and Eritrea. Its existence began in the 11th century, being established by Yekuno Amlak and up to 1974 when Haile Selassie, the then ruler of the kingdom was subverted in a coup d'état. The kingdom fought many wars to preserve its territory especially with the Italian Empire; however, it lost, and the Italian

Empire occupied it and established a colony of Italian East Africa in the area. Although the Ethiopian empire incorporated Eritrea into it in 1962, a civil war broke out in the empire causing Eritrea to gain independence and subsequently leading to the fall of the Ethiopian empire.

Sultanate of Ifat

The Sultanate of Ifat was a Muslim empire that existed between the 13th century through the 15th century in the east region of East Africa. The heart of the empire was a city called Zeila. The territories of the kingdom include eastern Ethiopia, Djibouti, and Somaliland of the modern day. In the early part of the 15th century, Emperor Dawit I defeated the then ruler of the empire and then destroyed the kingdom.

Hadiya Sultanate

The Hadiya Sultanate was an antediluvian empire that was based in southwestern Ethiopia; from the Abbay River, it is located south, and from Shewa, it is to the west. The land was fertile, its people grew cereals and fruits and owned horses, and iron was the empire's currency.

Sultanate of Mogadishu

The Mogadishu Sultanate is also called the Kingdom of Magadazo, and it was an ancient empire that was based in southern Somalia. It rose to be one of the empires to dominate the region of East Africa when it was being ruled by Fakhr ad-Din before it was incorporated into the Ajuran Empire in the 13th century. It had a large network of trade and had its own currency.

Kingdom of Buganda

Buganda kingdom is a kingdom of the Ganda people of Uganda, and it is the largest of the kingdoms in East Africa today. Before the 12th century, the kingdom was known as Muwaawa. However, the kingdom lost its independence to British rule and its adopted name became Uganda, which is the Swahili translation of Buganda. It regained its independence in 1962. It still is in existence today and is ruled by Queen Sylvia Nagginda.

Ajuran Sultanate

The Ajuran Empire was an empire in ancient times belonging to the Muslim Sultanate of Somalia which exercised dominance over East Africa. The government of the Sultanate was centralized, and it had a strong military to oppose foreign invasions. The empire was invested in architecture as it built castles and fortresses. The empire started to dwindle toward the end of the 17th century and this led to the rise of other Somalian powers.

Kingdom of Kaffa

The Kaffa Kingdom was an empire that was based in present-day Ethiopia, having Bonga as its offset capital. The kingdom had different groups of people living within its borders, such as the hunters called *Manje*, the leatherworkers, known as the *Manne*, and the blacksmiths called *Qemmo*. The kingdom was overcome and incorporated by Ethiopia in the year 1897.

Kingdom of Rwanda

The Rwanda Kingdom was a Bantu kingdom in the Horn of Africa that existed before colonial rule. Though it fell under the rule of German and Belgian colonists, it retained its monarchical system of government until the 1961 Rwandan Revolution.

Adal Sultanate

The Kingdom of Adal, also known as the Adal Sultanate, was a Muslim kingdom and Sultanate of Somalia in East Africa. The kingdom was founded by local people who occupied Zeila, and it attained its greatest height between 1415 to 1577. The empire lost the majority of its lands after the death of its ruler, Imam Ahmed; its fall resulted from internal disputes within the Afar tribes.

Ankole Kingdom

The Ankole kingdom was an antediluvian Bantu kingdom that was based in southwestern Uganda and faced Lake Edward from the east. Mugabe (Omugabe) was the name of the kingdom's ruler. The kingdom was annexed into the British Protectorate of Uganda.

Kingdom of Burundi

The kingdom of Burundi was an empire that was located in what is today the Republic of Burundi, in East Africa, precisely the region of the Great Lakes. The kingdom was established in the 17th century and it fell under the rulership of European colonists in the 19th century.

Kingdom of Kooki

Kooki was a traditional empire located in the modern-day Rakai District of Uganda. The year 1720 was the year the kingdom was established by two Bunyoro princes whose names were Bwowe and Kitayimbwa. It was annexed into the Buganda Kingdom in 1896.

Sultanate of the Geledi

The Geledi Sultanate was an empire that had dominance over East Africa in the latter part of the 17th century and the 19th century. At its height, the kingdom built up an army under the rulership of Mahmud Ibrahim, who was the Sultan of that time.

Sultanate of Aussa

The Sultanate of Aussa was a kingdom that was in eastern Ethiopia, precisely in the region of Afar between the 18th century and the 19th century. This empire was believed to be the leading monarchy of the people of Afar. In 1936, it was annexed into Italian East Africa.

Majeerteen Sultanate

The Majeerteen Sultanate was a kingdom of the Somalian people; it was based in East Africa. The sultanate exercised dominance over the majority of northern Somalia in the latter part of the 19th century and early 20th century.

Kingdom of Gomma

The kingdom of Gomma was a kingdom in the Gibe area of Ethiopia that rose to prominence in the 18th century. The heart of the kingdom was Agaro, bordered to the north by Limmu-Ennarea, to the west by Gumma, the south by Gera, and the east by Jimma.

Tooro Kingdom

A section of the Bunyoro people broke out of the Bunyoro kingdom, and those people finally established a kingdom of their own known as the Kingdom of Tooro in the 19th century, precisely in the year 1830. In 1876, the kingdom was annexed into Bunyoro-Kitara; however, it regained its independence in 1891.

Kingdom of Jimma

Jimma was among the kingdoms in the region of Gibe in Ethiopia that rose to prominence in the 19th century. It was bordered to the west by Limmu-Ennarea, to the east by the Sidamo Kingdom of Janjero; and to the south, the Gojeb River stood between the empire and the Kingdom of Kaffa.

Kingdom of Gumma

Gumma was a kingdom from the Gibe region in Ethiopia that rose to prominence in the 18th century. It shared its eastern borders with the bend of the Didessa River that stood between it and Limmu-Ennarea, which was located toward the northeast, and Gomma and Gera kingdoms toward the south.

Sultanate of Hobyo

The Sultanate of Hobyo was a kingdom of the people of Somalia located in northeastern and central Somalia and eastern Ethiopia of today. Yusuf Ali Kenadid founded the kingdom in 1807; he was the cousin of the Sultan of the Majeerteen Sultanate.

Kingdom of Karagwe

Karagwe was a kingdom that was part of the kingdoms of the Great Lakes in the Horn of Africa. It achieved prominence in the early part of the 19th century under the rulership of King Ndagara.

Kingdom of Unyanyembe

The kingdom of Unyanyembe was a kingdom that was established in the 19th century. The kingdom had two capital cities, which were Tabora and Kwihara. The empire had to endure the fight for power between Mnywasela and Mkasiwa.

Precolonial Kingdoms of West Africa

Kingdom of Ife

The Kingdom of Ife, also referred to as Ilé-Ifé, is an ancient kingdom in the southwest of Nigeria; it is currently located in Osun State. Ancient artwork from the kingdom, such as sculptures of stone, terracotta, and bronze, show that the kingdom existed around 1200 CE.

Kingdom of Nri

The Nri Kingdom was a kingdom located in present-day Nigeria. One-third of Igboland were under the political and religious rule of the kingdom, and the ruler of the kingdom was a priest-king bearing the title *Eze Nri*. The ruler handled both trade and diplomatic matters relating to the people, and he possessed divine authority in the sphere of religion. The influence of the kingdom waned with the rise of the Benin Empire.

Takrur

Takrur was an ancient kingdom in West Africa that was established in c. 800. The period of prosperity in the kingdom was sometime around the time the

Ghana Empire also boomed. In 1235, the kingdom started declining and was eventually overcome by the Mali Empire in the 1280s.

Bonoman

Bonoman was an Akan kingdom in ancient times. The kingdom was based in modern-day southern Ghana – specifically the Bono, Bono East, and Ahafo areas – and eastern Ivory Coast. Many believe it to be the place where the subgroups of Akan people originated. The rise of other Akan kingdoms brought about its downfall, especially since its people started deserting the kingdom.

Benin Empire

The kingdom of Benin was an ancient kingdom of West Africa located in modern-day southern Nigeria. The modern-day nation-state called Benin and this empire are different. The capital of the kingdom was Edo; currently, it is called Benin City in Edo State. It was established in the 11th century CE, and it stood until 1897 when it was incorporated into the British Empire.

Oyo Empire

The Oyo Empire was a kingdom located in present-day Benin and Western Nigeria; its territory spanned the whole of southwestern Nigeria and the western part of northcentral Nigeria. It was the largest state of the Yoruba people and one of the significant kingdoms of West Africa from the middle of the 7th century to the late 18th century.

Kingdom of Dagbon

Dagbon Kingdom was an ancient kingdom in Ghana, established by the Dagomba (Dagamba) people in the 11th century. During the prominent period of the kingdom's existence, its territory covered the Northern, Upper West, and Upper East areas of what is now Ghana.

Sultanate of Agadez

The Sultanate of Agadez was a kingdom of the Berbers based in the city of Agadez which is located on the southern borders of the Sahara Desert in the north-central part of Niger. The kingdom was founded in 1449 by the Tuareg and Hausa people to serve as a country store. The kingdom faced decline in both economic activity and population in the 17th century and finally, was conquered by the French in 1900.

Mamprugu Kingdom

This kingdom was founded in the 13th century by Naa Gbanwah at Pusiga, which is away from Bawku with only a few miles' distance. Its territories include the North-East, Northern, Upper East, and Upper West regions of Ghana and down to Burkina Faso.

Kwararafa Confederacy

Kwararafa Confederacy was a state having different ethnic groups that were based around the valley of the Benue River in present-day Nigeria. It was established to the southwest of the Bornu Empire; the kingdom became prominent before the year 1500. By the 17th century, the kingdom had various conflicts with neighboring kingdoms and declined to become a tributary in the 18th century.

Kingdom of Cayor

The Kingdom of Cayor was the most influential kingdom in West Africa between the years 1549 and 1879. It broke off from the Jolof Empire in present-day Senegal. The kingdom was incorporated into the

French Empire twice, first in 1868 and then again in 1879.

Kingdom of Dahomey

The kingdom of Dahomey was an African kingdom located in what is now the nation-state of Benin. The kingdom was founded in the early part of the 17th century, developing on the Plateau of Abomey amidst the Fon people. It was incorporated into the French colonial empire in 1904.

Wukari Federation

Wukari is a traditional land that succeeded Kwararafa. The kingdom currently lies in the south of the Benue River Basin, in Taraba State, Nigeria. The Jukun people came to settle in Wukari in the 17th century.

Asante Empire

The Asante Empire was an empire of the Akan people that was established in the late 17th century of what is now Ghana. The kingdom's territory stretched from Ashanti to include the Brong-Ahafo Region, Central Region, Eastern Region, and

Western Region of modern-day Ghana. It fell when it became part of the Gold Coast colony in 1902.

Kong Empire

The Kong Empire was an ancient kingdom that was established by the Dyula immigrants from the Mali Empire, which was declining at the time. The kingdom became prominent in the 1800s. The kingdom fell when it suffered an attack from Samori Ture in 1898.

Precolonial Kingdoms of Central Africa

Kingdom of Kongo

Kongo was a kingdom that was located in Central Africa in what is now northern Angola, the western region of DR Congo, the Republic of Congo, and the deep south of Gabon. At its height, the kingdom's territories spanned in the west from the Atlantic Ocean to the Kwango River in the east, and in the north from the Congo River to the Kwanza River in the south.

Sultanate of Bagirmi

The Sultanate of Bagirmi was a kingdom in the southeast of Lake Chad in Central Africa. The kingdom was established in either the year 1480 or the year 1552; the kingdom's capital city was Massenya that was to the north of the Chari River and near the border of modern-day Cameroon. The kingdom was incorporated into the Wadai Sultanate in 1871.

Luba Empire

The Luba Kingdom was a kingdom existing before Central Africa fell under colonial rule, established by

King Kongolo Mwamba in roughly 1585. At the height of the empire, the king was receiving tribute from about one million people. The kingdom fell not long after it was raided by invaders in search of slaves.

Kingdom of Ndongo

The Ndongo Kingdom was a kingdom that occupied present-day Angola. Not much is known about the kingdom; however, it was more or less a feudatory of the Kingdom of Kongo as suggested by oral tradition.

Anziku Kingdom

Another prior kingdom to colonial Central Africa was the Anziku Kingdom, also called the Teke Kingdom. The kingdom was located in what is now the Republic of Congo, Gabon, and the Democratic Republic of Congo. The Anziku people were in control of the copper mines in the northeast border of Kongo.

Kasanje Kingdom

The Kasanje Kingdom was established in the year 1620 by a band of mercenaries from Imbangala who had defected from the Portuguese army. The kingdom was named after the leader of the mercenaries; the people elected a king from one of the three clans that established the kingdom.

Kingdom of Matamba

The Matamba Kingdom was a kingdom that was in existence before the era of colonial Central Africa, located in a region currently called the Baixa de Cassanje of the Melanje Province of present-day Angola. This kingdom resisted the colonists of Portugal for many years before it was annexed into Angola.

Lunda Empire

Lunda kingdom was a kingdom whose ruler was called the Mwane-a- n'Gaange. At the pinnacle of its existence, the kingdom was in control of territories of about 186,000 square miles. Having great military strength, it conquered various tribes; however, it was invaded by the Chokwe in the 19th century, and the kingdom fell.

Kuba Kingdom

The Kuba Kingdom was a kingdom that started as a conglomerate of different Bushongo-speaking tribes; there was no central authority. However, in about 1625, Shyaam a-Mbul a Ngoong seized power from one of the tribe's leaders and then united the other tribes into one under his rule. The period of heyday in the kingdom was between the 17th century and the 19th century.

Mbunda Kingdom

The Kingdom of Mbunda was an empire that was based in present-day southeast Angola in west Central Africa. At its height, the kingdom had land that stretched from Mithimoyi in central Morocco to Cuando Cubango Province in the southeast, sharing a border with Namibia. It was conquered by Portugal in the year 1914 during the Kolongongo War.

Adamawa Emirate

The Adamawa Emirate was a kingdom that was based in Fombina, which is more or less the region of Adamawa and Taraba states in Nigeria today, the three northern provinces of Cameroon, some areas of Chad, and the Central African Republic. It was established by a commander of Usman dan Fodio by the name of Modibo Adama in 1809.

Yeke Kingdom

The Yeke Kingdom was a kingdom that did not stand for long, existing between 1856 to 1891. It is an empire of the people of Garanganze in Katanga, Democratic Republic of Congo. Although, in its short existence, it rose to prominence and had a territory that was around 300 million square miles.

Precolonial Kingdoms of South Africa

Mapungubwe Kingdom

The kingdom of Mapungubwe was a kingdom in South Africa that was located where the Shashe and Limpopo Rivers meet, south of Great Zimbabwe. The period of the kingdom's existence was around c. 1075 to c. 1220. It set the stage for development that eventually led to the establishment of the Kingdom of Zimbabwe.

Kingdom of Zimbabwe

The Kingdom of Zimbabwe was a Karanga or Shona kingdom that existed between c.1000 and c. 1450. The kingdom was located in modern-day Zimbabwe, and the name of its capital was Lusvingo; it emerged after the kingdom of Mapungubwe collapsed. Around 1430, Prince Nyatsimba Mutota left the kingdom to go establish a dynasty of his own; that dynasty rose to become the Kingdom of Mutapa, which eventually dominated the Kingdom of Zimbabwe.

Kingdom of Mutapa

The Mutapa Empire was a kingdom with land that spanned through present-day Zimbabwe, Zambia, Mozambique, and South Africa. A little after the establishment of the kingdom, its land stretched for most of the territories between Tavara and the Indian Ocean. The vulnerability of the kingdom to attack and economic manipulation, as well as internal disputes, led to the collapse of the kingdom.

Kingdom of Butua

The Kingdom of Butua was a kingdom located in modern-day southwestern Zimbabwe. It was a gold source for both Arab traders and traders from Portugal. The kingdom was in existence between c. 1450 and c. 1683.

Maravi Kingdom

The Maravi Kingdom was a kingdom that was established in the 3rd century. By the 16th century, it spanned across the borders of present-day Malawi, Mozambique, and Zambia. In its heyday, the lands of the kingdom stretched from the area of the Tonga and Tumbuka people (north) to the Lower Shire (south).

Merina Kingdom

The Kingdom of Merina, also known as the Kingdom of Madagascar, existed from c. 1540 to c. 1897. It was located outside the coast of Southeast Africa, and it exercised dominance over the majority of present-day Madagascar in the 19th century.

Rozvi Empire

The Rozvi Empire was established in 1684 on the Plateau of Zimbabwe around Changamire Dombo. A number of reasons led to the empire's collapse, including the hostility between the ruling dynasty and the allied kingdoms, which caused many to desert the empire; and, it suffered two major droughts from 1795 to 1800 and from 1824 to 1829.

Ndwandwe Kingdom

This was a kingdom whose people spoke Bantu-Nguni; combined with the Mthethwa, they became an important authority in Zululand of the modern-day by the 19th century. The kingdom was destroyed when its army was defeated at the Battle of Mblatuze River.

Mthethwa Empire

The Mthethwa Empire was a South African kingdom that rose to prominence in the 18th century from the south of Delagoa Bay and inland in southeast Africa. According to scholars, Nguni tribesmen descended from northern Natal and the Lubombo Mountains. The empire was replaced by the Zulu Kingdom.

Zulu Kingdom

The Kingdom of Zululand was a South African empire that stretched through the Indian Ocean coast from the Tugela River (south) to the Pongola River (north). In 1879, the kingdom exercised dominance over the majority of modern-day KwaZulu-Natal and Southern Africa. The kingdom fell to the British in the Battle of Ulundi.

Ndebele Kingdom

The Ndebele Kingdom was a kingdom in Southern Africa that was home to the Mthwakazi – the proto-Ndebele people. Bantu people arrived in the kingdom sometime later, and the kingdom became a place for the settlement of different cultures.

African kingdoms in the precolonial period also include the Sahelian kingdoms which are not included in this list. They are written under a different subtopic.

Chapter Two

THE KINGDOM OF KUSH

The Kingdom of Kush had its capital located in present-day Northern Sudan. Kush was a kingdom that formed from the much older region of Nubia that was already inhabited since c. 8,000 BCE and stretched from the upper Nile leading up to the Red Sea. The kingdom of Kush was instrumental in the political and cultural developments of the Northeastern part of Africa. The kingdom was in existence for over a thousand years.

The Kingdom of Kush was largely influenced by the Egyptians as archeological evidence from Egypt and Sudan proves that they in contact as far back as c. 3150 BCE to c. 2614 BCE. This was the earliest period of development of the Egyptian Dynasty. The earliest reference of Kush by the Egyptians was the attack on it led by the founder of the middle kingdom, Mentuhotep II, in the 21st century BCE. In fact, Kush, sometimes referred to as Nubia, was a colony under the rule of the new Kingdom of Egypt around the 16th century BCE. The colony of Kush was governed by an Egyptian viceroy. The Kingdom of Kush rose after the collapse of the Bronze Age and also the collapse of the new Kingdom of Egypt in c. 1070 BCE and had its capital in Napata, which is located today in central Sudan.

The Kingdom of Kush, under the rule of King Kashta (also known as the Kushite), invaded Egypt in the 8th century. After the invasion, the Kushite kings would become pharaohs of the "Twenty-Fifth Dynasty" of Egypt. They ruled Egypt for one century and were later expelled in c. 656 BCE by the Psamtik. The capital of Kush Kingdom was later moved to Monroe, which according to Greek geographers was known as Aethiopia. It lasted until the 4th century CE before its disintegration caused by internal revolts. The kingdom is believed to be the most famous and long-lasting civilization that rose from Nubia, all through its existence of about three thousand years, and had its capital located in first Kerma, Napata, and lastly Meroe (or Monroe).

The kingdom of Kush was very wealthy, as every part of the kingdom contributed to its wealth. During its occupation by the Egyptians, Kush served as the main source of gold. Kush and later the Kingdom of Kush was called several names by different people. Because the region supplied gold to Egypt, some historians claimed that Nubia was derived from "nub," which is the Egyptian word for gold. Although the Egyptians also had another name for the region, which was Ta-Nehsy, meaning the "land of the black people." Kush was also referred to as "Aethiopia," which meant the "land inhabited by the people with a burnt face." And to the Arabs, it was known as Bilad al-Sudan, which meant "land of the black."

Kerma and Early Kush

The city of Kerma, which became the first capital of the kingdom of Kush, was founded in c. 2400 BCE. The city was built around a fortified religious center known as a "deffufa." It was built with mud bricks and had a height of fifty-nine feet. The worship center had several inner passageways alongside stairs that led to the altar located at the roof. This alter was where ceremonies were conducted, although little is known about the details of these ceremonies. There were smaller deffufa to the west and to the east (which is the smallest), and together, they formed a triad. This religious center triad became the center upon which the city was built and walls constructed around the city.

From Egyptian inscriptions and evidence of fortified buildings built to the south of Egypt to defend it against enemies, Kerma was an acknowledged rival. Despite this, there were trade relations between

Kerma and Egypt. Egypt's influx of goods such as ebony, gold, incense, ivory, animals, and so forth, was dependent on imports from Kerma. The Kushites, together with the Hyksos and Egyptians, had a tripartite trade relation in the region of Thebes. These trade relations were ended by the invasion and expulsion of the Hyksos by the Egyptians, who felt threatened by the military might of the people. This expedition was led by Ahmose I, who ruled Egypt from c. 1570 BCE to 1544 BCE. After Hyksos, he turned his attention to the Kushites. Egypt's attack on the Kushites continued under the reign of both Thutmose I and Thutmose III, who ruled from 1520 to 1492 BCE and 1458 to 1425 BCE, respectively. After Thutmose III successfully defeated and sacked Kerma, he established the city of Napata to consolidate the power of Egypt in the entire region. C. 1500 BCE is generally held as the year Kerma collapsed.

Napata

As seen above, Napata was the creation of the Egyptians, and as such, from its onset, it was greatly influenced by Egyptian culture. Thutmose III, after establishing Napata, built close to the mountain of Jebel Barkal, the great temple of Amun. This temple became the most outstanding religious center throughout the history of the Kushites. Other Egyptian pharaohs, such as Ramesses II, contributed to the architecture of the temple. Subsequent autonomous Kushite kings were religiously under the control of the priests of Amun just the same way their former hegemony, Egyptian pharaohs, were since the era of the Old Kingdom.

The New Kingdom of Egypt began to decline in c. 1069. This decline was partly a result of the struggle for power between the priests of Amun and the pharaoh, which resulted in the separation of the kingdom's political administration. The priests of Amun at Thebes gained much power from c. 1069 to 525 BCE. This period was known as Egypt's Third Intermediate Period. During this period, Egypt was divided into Upper and Lower Egypt. The High Priest of Amun had political control of Upper Egypt while the pharaoh only had political control over Lower Egypt. As Egypt grew weak, Kush was gaining strength, and Napata gradually grew into an independent political entity. Egypt could no longer maintain its sovereignty over it as it had internal crises to deal with. Many scholars mark c. 1069 BCE as the birth date of the kingdom of Kush because it was when the Kushite rulers began to reign autonomously, free from interference from Egyptian politics or monarchs. Although the kingdom of Kush was now autonomous, they still maintained trade relations with Egypt and neighboring nations. But now, they dictated the terms as they saw fit. For quite some time, the royal necropolis remained in Kerma, the kingdom's first capital, and kings had to be buried there until it was moved to Napata. The kingdom of Kush grew mightily to the point of having the powers to oppress its former oppressors. But every time they would enter Egypt it was to preserve and defend Egyptian culture and not to conquer it. A typical example was the Twenty-Fifth Dynasty.

The Twenty-Fifth Dynasty

King Alara took advantage of the opportunity presented by the decline in Egyptian power and wealth during the Third Intermediate Period. He unified the kingdom under the capital of Napata. Although there are no documented dates for him, he was a very popular king among the people of Kush. Evidence of his rule can be found in inscriptions that were discovered on what appears to be his tomb. He laid a very good foundation for his successor Kashta. Under Kashta's reign, Napata and the entire kingdom of Kush was "Egyptianized." He imported numerous Egyptian artifacts for decoration and religious purposes to the kingdom.

Kashta had a very good relationship with the priests of Amun in Thebes who controlled Upper Egypt. He capitalized on this relationship and had his daughter, who was named Amenirdis I, chosen as the wife of the gods. The wife of the gods is a position held by a woman who had the same political powers and wealth as the High Priest of Amun. This was a very important position in Egyptian society. All of this was made possible because of the persistent decline of the powers of the pharaoh after losing their rule over Upper Egypt. Kashta then used his daughter to usurp the powers of the High Priest and gained control of Thebes. With control over Thebes, he seized control over the whole of Upper Egypt. Again, the princes who were fighting among themselves could not interfere. With his daughter controlling Upper Egypt and disunity among members of the ruling class in Lower Egypt, Kashta declared himself king of all Egypt. He was successful and established what is now called in history the Twenty-Fifth Dynasty of Egypt without using military force. Piye, who was Kashta's son, succeeded him from c. 747 to 721 BCE.

When Piye ascended the throne, he enforced Kushite rule over Upper and Lower Egypt. Though he met little resistance from the princes who were weak and divided, he deployed his army and subdued every city in Lower Egypt. After establishing his sovereignty, he then returned home to Napata. He restored existing kings and consolidated their authority to rule as it has always been. The only thing Piye requested was for them to recognize him as "lord." Piye never occupied Egypt. At his death, his brother Shabaka became king from c. 721 to 707 BCE, and he continued in his brother's footsteps. Shabaka also allowed the indigenous kings of Egypt to maintain their autonomy so long as they recognized his sovereignty. Like his brother, he too remained and ruled from the capital of Kush, Napata. Shabaka was also a lover of the Egyptian culture like his brother and father before him. During his rule, it is believed that the "Egyptianization" of the kingdom was so deep to the extent that when King Shabaka marched into Lower Egypt to suppress the rebellion of the princes and finally imposed the Nubian culture on the Egyptians, scholars say he was only still imposing Egyptian culture on the Egyptians. Shabaka consolidated his rule by making Haremakhet, his son, appointed as the High Priest of Amun. Shabaka, contrary to some beliefs, preserved Egyptian culture.

Shabaka was succeeded by Shebitku, his nephew from c. 707 to 690 BCE. Under his reign, the kingdom of Kush and its colony Egypt continued to flourish. Shebitku, like his uncle, continued to give asylum to rebel leaders who escaped Assyria in Mesopotamia. For example, the kingdom of Kush gave sanctuary to Ashdod, the leader of the revolution against King Sargon of Assyria. This caused the Assyrians to attack Egypt in 671 BCE during the reign of Shebitku's successor, King Taharqa. King Taharqa was defeated, captured and taken to Nineveh alongside his family and other Kushite and Egyptian royals. King Taharqa escaped to Napata. Tantamani succeeded him from c. 669 BCE to 666 BCE, and continued to support rebels against Assyria. Egypt was finally conquered in 666 BCE, and this ended the Twenty-Fifth Dynasty.

City of Meroe

After the Assyrians defeated the king of the Kingdom of Kush and took over Egypt, they placed over its affairs Pharaoh Necho I, who was succeeded by Psamtik I, his son, from 665 to 610 BCE. During the reign of Psamtik, Egypt was liberated from the Assyrians. This marked the beginning of the Twenty-Sixth Dynasty. After his death, Necho II succeeded him, and he led an attack on the Kingdom of Kush. Pharaoh Necho II sacked Kush's capital city of Napata as well as other towns, monuments, temples, and so forth, and although Necho II was successful, he did not occupy the kingdom but pulled back his troops and returned to Egypt. In c. 590 BCE, after the destruction of Napata, the King of Kush moved the capital of the kingdom to a city called Meroe. In Meroe, the Kingdom of Kush continued to follow the same culture, religion, and administrative system as the Egyptians. But when Arkamana I ascended the throne in c. 295 BCE and ruled until 275 BCE, he refuted the Egyptian customs and pattern of administration. It is believed that the king was schooled in Greek philosophy, hence he decided to do away with the absurd beliefs of the people that were upheld by the priests of Amun. Hitherto, the priests of Amun ultimately controlled the Kings of Kush the same way it was in the Egyptian society. The priests had the power to change the monarch and force the former to commit suicide. This, the High Priest did by merely declaring the gods did not want the ruler anymore. Arkamani I abolished the priest's powers over the kings by killing all the priests of Amun.

During the reign of Arkamani I, the Kingdom of Kush saw the institution of new practices and customs different to and independent of those practiced in Egypt. The kingdom found its own identity under Arkamani I. Among the things that changed was the hitherto Egyptian fashion style to

Meroitic fashion, hieroglyphic script to Meroitic script. Also, the gods became known as Apademak, an indigenous deity of the Kushites. Arkamani I, for the first time in the history of the Kushites, established the right of female monarchs known as Kandake to rule. Although for public ceremonies, these queens had to be accompanied by a male figure. These queens ruled from c. 284 BCE to 314 BCE and the first ever recorded queen was Shanakdakhete in c. 170 BCE. Another queen was Amanirenas from c. 40 BCE to 10 BCE. She led the Kushites into battle during the Meroitic war against Rome, which lasted from 27 BCE to 22 BCE. Rome at that time was under the reign of Augustus Caesar. Queen Amanirenas was able to secure for her people a peace treaty that was favorable.

Economy

The kingdom of Kush, like its ancient Nubian culture, was cosmopolitan. The region has always served as one of the major trading centers connecting the Arabian Desert, Mediterranean basin, and African interior. Nubians imported goods such as timber, incense, bronze, jewelry, stone vessels, wine, olive oil, and clothes from Egypt, the Mediterranean basin, and the Maghreb. The Nubians traded ebony, gold, ivory, hides, ostrich eggs, live animals (such as elephants, giraffes, monkeys, etc.). The Nubian communities were strategic because they opened up to the Red Sea on the east. The Red Sea was a preferred and better avenue for sailing long distances when compared to the Nile. Sometimes, the king of Kush would demand processed goods in exchange for raw materials. The kingdom of Kush played a very important role in the Afro-Eurasian global system where ideas, goods, and even people would be exchanged.

Chapter Three

THE LAND OF PUNT

The Land of Punt, described as "the land of the gods" in ancient Egyptian text, is a region rich in resources. In the year 1822 CE, after Jean-Francois Champollion first deciphered Egyptian hieroglyphics, scholars around the world, after studying the text, began to question as to where the Land of Punt is located today and what could be its modern name. Based on the evidence found from the inscriptions in the deciphered text, it is believed that the Land of Punt is the modern-day Puntland state of Somalia. According to historian Ahmed Abdi, the city of Pouen referenced as part of Punt by ancient inscriptions is identical to the ancient city of Opone in Somalia. The Land of Punt was known as *Pwenet* or *Pwene* to the Egyptians, which is translated as "Pouen." Pouen to the Greek is known as Opone. It is no secret that Opone traded with Egypt many centuries ago.

The Land of Punt is famously known for the expedition of Queen Hatshepsut in 1493 BCE in the Eighteenth Dynasty of Egypt. This brought about the successful first attempt in transplanting foreign fauna as a result of the exchange between Egypt and Punt, which brought back living trees to Egypt. Though this voyage to Punt is famously known, evidence shows that the Egyptians had been trading with the Land of Punt as far back as the Fourth Dynasty (c. 2613–2498 BCE) during Pharaoh Khufu's reign.

Egypt as a nation grew, and in the latter part of the Predynastic period (c. 6000–3150 BCE), trade increased also. The early Dynastic period brought about the firm establishment of trade with Mesopotamia and Phoenician regions. Through trade, Egypt by the Fifth Dynasty (c. 2498–2345) in the Phoenician city of Byblos, and the countries of Punt and Nubia began to flourish. Punt became a major source of cultural and religious influence in as much as it played a major role in trade. It is a land that the Egyptians considered blessed by the gods and a place of their origin.

Location

Among archaeologists, scholars, historians, and others, there exists disputes as to the current location of the Land of Punt. Although over the years, places like present-day Somalia or the Puntland State of Somalia at the Horn of Africa, a part of Arabia, Eritrea, Sudan, or even some regions of East Africa, have been cited to be the exact location of the Land of Punt. Among these places debated by historians and scholars alike, Eritrea and Somalia are the most likely, with Eritrea coming out top since it gained the most acceptance.

However, judging from the expedition of Hatshepsut carved on the temple at Deir al-Bahri, it would seem that the present-day Puntland State of Somalia is the location of the Land of Punt.

Historian Abdisalam Mahamoud is of the view that the ancient Somali name for their region was "Bunn," which is a name referring to the trade with Egypt as "Pwene" or "Pwenet." This region is known in the present day as "Bunni." From the culture of the Puntland State of Somalia, one can see a similarity in language, ceremonial dress, and arts to that of ancient Egypt.

According to Hatshepsut's inscriptions, it is believed that her mother hailed from Punt. There are also inscriptions pointing Egyptians of the Eighteenth Dynasty to Punt. These Egyptians considered Punt as the source of the origin of their culture. Being intrigued by how proud Hatshepsut was of her expedition to Punt, the scholar John A. Wilson seems to favor Somalia as Punt when he points out the "usual prominence" of this expedition. In his writing, John A. Wilson indicated that it was "the land of incense to the south, perhaps chiefly in the Somaliland area, but also Arabia Felix." There is no way Punt could be in Arabia or Nubia because the Egyptians regularly traded with it, and it was not "to the south"; neither is it the latter since the Egyptians knew that land all too well, and there is nothing "mysterious" about it. Trade conducted via sea travel is also an indication that both Arabia and Nubia are not the Land of Punt. The region of Eritrea seems to be the best contender for Punt since the high possibility that the Land of Punt is located above Somalia and Eritrea fits the bill.

Due to other expeditions and the description of Hatshepsut, some persons favor Somalia as the Land of Punt since the Egyptians traveled there by boat down River Nile, via the Wadi Tumilat in the eastern Delta down to the Red Sea. Evidence also exists that shows the Egyptian crews that visited Punt disassembling their boat and carrying them overland to the Red Sea, hugging the shores as they made their way to Punt. In as much as this description seems to favor an interpretation of Eritrea, the evidence in favor of Somalia is weightier. According to Wilson's pointing to the evidence found at Hatshepsut's temple, the people of the Land of Punt were so thrilled at the arrival of the Egyptians even though it seems like they were living at the edge of the world. Wilson writes:

> The people of Punt are flatteringly amazed at the boldness of the Egyptian sailors: "How did you reach here, the country unknown to men? Did you come down on the ways of heaven, or did you travel by land or sea? How happy God's Land (Punt), which you now tread like Ra!"

Another scholar Marc van de Mieroop, while describing how foreign the Land of Punt was to the Egyptians, writes:

> The Egyptians reached Punt by seagoing boat and found it a country very unlike their own. The representations of houses, animals, and plants suggest a location in northeast Africa along the Red Sea coast, possibly the region of modern Eritrea, although a local farther inland has also been suggested.

Archaeologist Dr. Juris Zarins presented more compelling evidence linking the Land of Punt to Somalia when he argued that during the Neolithic period, settlers from the River Nile valley took over the region of Somalia, and the two years were dominated by trade as early as the second millennium BCE. Dr. Juris Zarins's claim is equally backed up by ancient architectural and cultural evidence strongly linking Punt to Somalia.

Hatshepsut's Expedition to Punt

In as much as trade has been ongoing between the Egyptians and the people of Punt, Hatshepsut's 1493 BCE expedition to Punt holds a special meaning. The reason could be that Hatshepsut's transaction with the Land of Punt was somewhat on a grand scale. However, evidence suggested that Hatshepsut was directed by the gods on how to establish the right connection to Punt after she had lost her way. Based on the reliefs from Hatshepsut temple, the scholar, Wilson, has been able to describe how the voyage was commissioned:

> Amun-Ra of Karnak spoke from his sanctum in the temple and directed Hatshepsut to undertake the commercial exploration of the land of Punt. "The majesty of the palace made petition at the stairs of the Lord of the Gods. A command was heard from the Great Throne, an oracle of the god himself, to search out ways to Punt, to explore the roads to the terraces of myrrh."

Making room for the will of the gods, five ships were prepared solely for the journey with lots of goods gathered for trade. Based on the inscriptions from Hatshepsut's reign, Historian Barbara Watterson describes the journey as:

> Five ships en route from a port on the Red Sea (possibly Quseir) set out to journey southwards to Suakin, where the expedition disembarked. The voyage had taken between 20 and 25 days, covering on average about 50 kilometers a day, with the ships hugging the coast rather than risk the dangerous deep water of the Red Sea. From Suakin, the route to Punt was overland through the Red Sea hills.

The description of this journey to Punt by land following through the passing of the Red Sea could be a major contender for Eritrea or Somalia as long as the other pieces of evidence are taken into consideration. The houses at Punt are set on stilts, and the people of Punt are governed by a king who had elders as his advisers. According to inscriptions, the people of Punt were described as being extremely generous, and the relations between Punt and Egypt were very good. Egyptian scribes have never been shy of their praise for the Land of Punt, for its riches and "goodness."

Egypt, Punt, and Trade

A relief from the Fourth Dynasty has shown one of Pharaoh Khufu's sons with a Puntite, and documents from the Fifth Dynasty have shown both countries enriching themselves through regular trade. An inscription from military commander Pepynakht Heqalb, who served under King Pepy II (2278–2184 BCE) of the Sixth Dynasty, told of how he was sent by King Pepy II to "the Land of Aamu" to retrieve the body of Kekhen, the warden who was killed by the Aamu and the Sand-dwellers when he was building a reed boat from the Land of Aamu to travel to Punt. The Sand-dwellers were from Sudan, while the Aamu were Asiatics of Arabia contending for the port of Suakin (as earlier noted by Watterson) for a departure point for Egyptian trade on the west coast of the Red Sea. The trade with Punt was needed by the Egyptians for many of Punt's prized possessions.

Ebony, gold, wild animals, elephant tusks, ivory, spices, precious woods, animal skins, cosmetics, incense, myrrh trees, and frankincense were the items brought to Egypt from Punt. Historian Barbara Watterson writes: "In return for a modest present of a few Egyptian weapons and some trinkets, the Puntites gave their visitors sacks of aromatic gum, gold, ebony, ivory, leopard skins, live apes, and incense trees." From Watterson's description, it might seem that the trade between both countries was one-sided, but with the inscription, we saw a fair-trade exchange between both countries. Wilson, while reporting how the Egyptians arrived at Punt, writes with "jewelry, tools, and weapons" and returned with "incense trees, ivory, myrrh, and rare woods." Evidence also suggests that Egyptians, having their own gold mines traded metals from their country for Punt's gold.

As stated earlier, the fauna (plants and trees), being an impressive article of trade, was successfully transplanted in another country during Egyptian trade with Punt. The fauna, being the first time in history its transplant had happened in another soil, was not only successful, it even flourished for centuries in Egypt. Outside the Hatshepsut complex at Deir al-Bahri, the root of the Frankincense tree brought from her expedition to Punt in 1493 BCE can still be seen. According to the inscriptions found on the wall of the site, Egyptians and the people of Punt held each other in deep respect, and the trade between both countries was mutually beneficial. Also, there exists evidence from the temple that shows the envoys from Egypt being received with honor by the Puntite chief and his wife. So vivid was the description that scholars and historians have been able to diagnose the Puntite wife of Chief Aty's medical challenges. Historian Jimmy Dunn writes that the queen "shows signs of lipodystrophy or Dercum's disease. She had a pronounced curvature of the spinal column." A segment of the inscriptions referenced Perehu, who was a king of Punt at that time, and his generosity, which was seen in the vast goods brought back to Egypt. In as much as the reign of Queen Hatshepsut was one of the most prosperous in the history of Egypt, nothing trumps her expedition to Punt. Watterson, explaining the inscriptions found at the queen's temple at Deir al-Bahri, writes of how important Punt was to the queen: "Reliefs depicting important themes from Hatshepsut's life decorate walls in the colonnades: her birth, the transportation of obelisks for the Temple of Amun in Thebes, the great expedition to Punt."

Marc van de Mieroop also lends his own voice to this comment by saying: "Complete incense trees as well as loose incense, an expensive fragrant tree extract that was used in religious services as an offering to the gods" were among the goods imported. The expedition gathered a large amount of it (incense), and the accompanying inscription describes how those quantities were never acquired before. How prominent the relief was, shows the pride that Hatshepsut awarded the achievements of her expedition.

In addition to the valuable things mentioned above, thirty-one incense trees (Boswellia) were also brought back to Egypt from Punt, which made the visit of Punt as important as the goods traded there.

Egypt's legendary past and gods have a strong affiliation with the Land of Punt since some of the materials used in the Egyptian temple for rituals were obtained from Punt. For instance, the leopard skin worn by the priest, the gold used in the sanctuary, and the incense burned in the temple were from Punt. It is believed that the gods that shower the Land of Egypt with their goodness had like affection for the Land of Punt. Evidence suggests that the dwarf-god, known as the "god of childbirth," was equally from Punt. The same is said of other gods of Egypt (with Hatshepsut's mother, Hathor not excluded), all having Punt as their origin.

Legend of Punt and the Modern Day

Punt became immortalized in the Egyptian literature during the Twelfth Dynasty (1991–1802 BCE) as the popular tale of a castaway Egyptian sailor who was shipwrecked on an island, finding himself conversing with a serpent that calls itself the "Lord of Punt."

The great serpent aided the Egyptian sailor in locating his way back to Egypt, laden with spices, gold, and unique animals. The sailor, on arriving home, tells his master of his encounter with the great serpent in order to encourage him after a failed expedition, knowing how disappointed his master must feel since he himself had encountered worse — fearing for his life and losing his ship also.

Since the Land of Punt had been linked with the gods in the past, it was intentionally chosen in this tale as the mystical island the sailor was washed up upon. The sailor's message to his master was simple, and it is that even in the darkest moment of one's life, when life looks bleak, and it seems like all hope is lost, good can still happen. This, the sailor did by reminding his master and anyone who would later hear of the tale of the gods and their blessings by pointing to the fact that his voyage that was doomed for failure ended up enriching him with the "Lord of Punt" turning his fortunes around.

Through the New Kingdom (1570–1069 BCE), the Land of Punt that until then was a semi-mythical land to the Egyptians became a very real place. Tributes from foreign delegates to the Land of Punt were accepted by the Vizier, Rekhmira, in the reign of Amunhotep II (1425–1400 BCE). Punt was equally mentioned during the reign of Ramesses II the Great (1279–1213 BCE) and Ramesses III (1186–1155 BCE). The Egyptians became so fascinated with the Land of Punt and have come to know her as a "Land of Plenty," calling Punt Te Netjer, the land of the gods, from which every good thing comes to Egypt. Punt, on the other hand, came to see the Land of Egypt as their ancient homeland, having associated with Egyptian ancestry, calling it the land where the gods emerged from and consorted with each other. The Land of Punt that was so exalted from reality into mythology came to a decline in the minds of Egyptians after the reign of Ramesses III until it was lost both in legend and folklore.

Today, the people of Somalia still keep the customs and language of ancient Egypt alive as a way of honoring their relationship with the people of Egypt. Citing English linguist Charles Barber, historian Abdislam Mahamoud describes how the language of ancient Egypt came from the Hamitic group of languages still spoken "across a large part of North Africa including Somali." Mahamoud, referencing this citing, commented on how people in modern-day Somalia continue naming their children after ancient Egyptian gods – for instance, being called in modern-day language "Oraxthy" from the ancient Egyptian "Horakhty." Even though the Land of

Punt may have slowly disappeared into mythology in ancient Egypt, its rich heritage is still being preserved by those in the present day who choose to remember their past and honor it.

Chapter Four

CARTHAGE

The Carthage city founded on the coast of northwest Africa in the 9th century BCE is located in present-day Tunisia, being one of the Phoenician settlements in the Western Mediterranean, created for the purpose of facilitating trade from the city of Tyre, Sidon, and others on the coast of present-day Lebanon. Throughout the Mediterranean, Carthage developed into a major trading empire with both its name and city coming into the limelight. Though there is no significant data attesting to when Carthage became an independent power, neither is there anything that can distinguish Carthage from other colonies in the Northwest region of Africa and the Mediterranean during 800–700 BCE. Carthage's commercial value shot to the limelight at the end of the 7th century BCE when it was fast becoming the leading commercial center of the West Mediterranean region. After the Punic Wars (the long conflict with the emerging Roman Republic in 264–146 BCE), Carthage was finally destroyed by Rome in 146 BCE, with its water supply cut off, its walls torn down, and its harbor rendered unusable following its defeat at the hand of the Arab invaders at the end of 7th century. Tunis later became the major regional center that replaced Carthage and has expanded to include the ancient site of Carthage as a modern suburb.

Originally, Carthage was known as Kart-hadasht (new city) in order to distinguish it from the older Phoenician city of Utica nearby. While the Greeks call it Karchedon, the Romans turned this name into Carthage. It was founded by the Legendary Queen Dido in 814 BCE, and it expanded following the conquest of Alexander the Great (332 BCE) with the immigration of refugees from the city of Tyre. It continued expanding until it became the seat of the Carthaginian Empire with colonies (such as Sabratha) along the North Africa regions, in Sicily and Spain. These were lost as a result of the Punic Wars, which saw Rome take Carthage's former position as the greatest Mediterranean power.

Into five periods was the history of the ancient city of Carthage divided. They are Ancient Carthage (Punic Republic) in 814–146 BCE, Roman Carthage in 146 BCE to 439 CE, Vandal Carthage in 439–534 CE, Byzantine Carthage (Exarchate of Africa) in 534–698 CE, and the Muslim Arab Carthage (Islamic Carthage) in 698–1270 CE.

The ancient city of Carthage was conquered and destroyed in the period 698 BCE during the Arab Muslim invasion of North Africa. In as much as it was later rebuilt, though, to a moderate scale, it was finally destroyed under Muhammad I al-Mustansir's reign (r. 1228–1277 CE), after conquering the European Christian invasion of the Eighth Crusade of 1270 CE. Though still inhabited, its ancient ruins were left that way until when modern excavations began in the 1830s CE.

Foundation and Expansion

Legend has it that the Phoenician Queen Elissa (better known as Dido) founded Carthage in c. 814 BCE. Dido, while running away from the tyranny of her brother Pygmalion of Lebanon, found herself in the region of North Africa. There, she established the city on the high hill that was later known as Byrsa. The legend further lets us know that the Berber chieftain, who was the overseer of that region, told Dido that she could have as many lands as an ox hide can take. So, Dido got an ox hide and cut them into smaller pieces laying them end to end to claim the island for herself and her people.

According to the Roman poet Virgil (l. 70–19 BCE) and other accounts, Dido's reign was described as impressive, taking into consideration how the city that was a small community on the hill grew into a gigantic metropolis. This was so legendary that Carthage, which seems to be a minor spot where the Phoenician traders would stop to either repair their ship or restock their supply, became a major trade center in the 4th century BCE.

In 332 BCE, the city developed significantly following Alexander's destruction of the great industrial and trade center of Tyre (known as Carthage's mother-city) with Phoenician refugees fleeing to Carthage with all manner of wealth they had left since Alexander only spared those of rich means. These men coming to Carthage with their wealth only enforced the city as the new center of Phoenician trade.

Not wasting any time, the Carthaginians quickly established a working relationship with the Masaesyli tribes and the Massylii of the North Africa Berber (Imazighen) Kingdom of Numidia, who would occupy the ranks of their military, forming a formidable cavalry. From a small town on a hill, Carthage soon became the richest and most powerful city in the Mediterranean with large estates covering large acreage of lands.

By the 4th century BCE, Carthage's government, which was formerly a monarchy, became a republic-based meritocracy (a system where the elite of the society rules) with two elected magistrates known as Suffetes ("judges") occupying the top position. The Suffetes were to govern alongside a senate of between two hundred to three hundred members who would occupy that position for life. The assembly of citizens would vote on the measures put forward by the Suffetes and senate; only then would the law be passed. The lowest in the society lived in huts or apartments outside the city. The middle-class lived in beautiful and attractive homes while the aristocrats had their dwellings in the palace.

Apart from the major lucrative business in maritime trade, money also came in through tariffs and tributes. These also helped in boosting the economy of Carthage. The city harbor was properly immense, having a gleaming column in a half-circle around it with capacity for 220 ships. In front of it were towering arches and buildings designed with Greek sculptures. The two harbors that existed in the city were for trade and resupplying, repairing and outfitting warship vessels. Around the Mediterranean Sea, the Carthaginian trading ships sailed daily to ports, with their navy ensuring their people were safe by keeping guard of the water and also conquering new territories for trade and resources, which in turn extended Carthage boundaries all the more.

Carthage had four residential sections, which were around Byrsa acting as a stronghold at the center, surrounded by walls stretching twenty-three miles in length from the inland of the harbor. Just like any great city, Carthage had a theater for entertainment, a temple for religious activities, a necropolis, a marketplace that was very grand, beautiful accommodation structures and refinements. The goddess of love and fertility, Tanit, alongside her consort Baal-Hamon were the patron deities of Carthage. Though this claim has been challenged, it was purported that children were sacrificed to Tanit in the sacred precinct of Tophet. It is possible that the Tophet of Carthage city was simply a necropolis kept for infants and the young.

Affluence and Invasion

The wealth of Carthage was not only because of how well they were positioned on the North Africa coast, which put them in a very advantageous position in controlling traffic at sea between the city and Sicily. The wealth of Carthage can also be pointed to its people's skills in agriculture. The author of Mago of Carthage wrote a comprehensive twenty-eight volume book that was devoted to the science of agriculture and veterinarian study, which simply reflects the intense interest of the Carthaginians in farming and animal husbandry at the time. Mago's work was so significant that they were among the few spared by the Romans in 146 BCE after the final defeat of Carthage. Now all that remains from that work are just a few references from the Romans.

The Carthaginians planted vegetables, olive trees, grapes, and fruit trees and then expanded cultivation all the way to the field of grains. Carthage continued to flourish as the city's wealth through trade with the interior as well as maritime trade elsewhere increased through their expertise in cultivation and the fertility of the land.

The first conflict the city of Carthage ever experienced with others was as a result of their expansion. North Africa was invaded in 310–307 BCE by Agathocles of Syracuse (r. 317–289 BCE), who sought Carthage wealth for war. Though Agathocles was able to feed his men from the rich crops that grew in abundance on the land, he was defeated because the Libyans and Berbers who worked the land were on the side of the Carthaginians since the Carthaginians were agreeable to them. So, Agathocles and his men were driven from North Africa. In 264 BCE, Carthage became involved in a conflict with Rome, which was a small city-state on the Tiber River in Italy.

The Punic Wars

The conflict with Rome began over the control of Sicily since it was now divided between Rome and Carthage and their support for the opposing factions on the island quickly brought both parties against each other. This conflict is what later led to what we call the Punic Wars today. When compared to Carthage, Rome posed no threat as it was weak and the Carthaginian navy in the past had successfully been able to keep the Romans from trading west of the Mediterranean.

To Carthaginians' surprise, Rome proved to have far more resources than Carthage could imagine when the First Punic War began in 264–241 BCE. Rome, with no navy and no idea of fighting on the sea, quickly built 330 ships, equipping them with gangways and ingenious ramps that could be lowered into an enemy ship to secure it. After a series of military tactics, Rome came out on top, causing Carthage to cede Sicily and thereby pay a heavy price. Carthage was defeated by Rome in 241 BCE.

In 241–237 BCE, immediately after the war, Carthage became drawn into what is known as the

Mercenary War. This was when the Carthaginian mercenaries were demanding that the debt owed to them be paid. Carthage won the Mercenary War with the help of general Hamilcar Barca (I. c. 285–c. 228 BCE).

Carthage suffered greatly in the aftermath of the First Punic and the Mercenary War, and even when Rome occupied Carthaginian colonies of Sardinia and Corsica, there was nothing the Carthaginians could do about it. Making the best of what they now had seemed to be the best idea. This Carthage did, which led them to go to war again with Rome when they tried to expand their holdings in Spain by attacking an ally of Rome known as the city of Saguntum in 218 BCE. The attack was led by Hannibal.

In 218–202 BCE, the Second Punic War was fought in Northern Italy. Hannibal marching his troops into the Alps, invaded Italy from Spain, and he won every engagement with the Romans in Italy. In 216 BCE, Hannibal came out victorious at the Battle of Cannae but, due to insufficient supplies and troops, he could not build on his successes. He was finally drawn from Italy at the battle of Zama in North Africa in 202 BCE and was defeated by the Roman general Scipio Africanus (l. 236–183 BCE). This led to Carthage suing for peace again and Rome placing

Carthage again under a heavy war indemnity. Carthage, not enjoying the spoils of war, was battling to pay off their debt while also trying to fend off an attack from their neighbors, Numidia, an ally of Rome during the Second Punic War under King Masinissa (r. c. 202–148 BCE). Numidia was encouraged by Rome to raid the Carthaginians at will. As such, the Carthaginians went to war against King Masinissa of Numidia, and in so doing, broke the peace treaty they had with the Romans. The peace treaty stated that the Carthaginians were forbidden to mobilize an army, and that was what they did against Numidia. According to Rome's sanction, Carthage now had to pay a war debt to Numidia after they just came out of one with Rome. Even though Carthage felt that they had no choice but to defend themselves against Numidia, Rome wasn't concerned, neither were they pleased with Carthage for revitalizing their military.

Carthage thinking that their treaty with Rome ended when they paid off their debt was greatly mistaken as Rome did not see it as so. The Romans still wanted to bend Carthage to do their bidding that the Roman senator Cato Elder in all his speeches, no matter the subject, always ended with the phrase "Further, I think Carthage must be destroyed." In 149 BCE,

Rome decided upon that course of action, and Carthage was destroyed.

The Roman embassy to Carthage stipulated that Carthage be dismantled completely and then rebuilt further inland, all in an attempt to render its once-held position and long-standing advantage over trade on the coast unrecognizable. To this effect, the Carthaginians refused, and this led to the Third Punic War in 149–146 BCE.

For three years, the Roman general, Scipio Aemilianus (l. 185–129 BCE) besieged Carthage until it fell. After ransacking it, the Romans burned the city to the ground leaving no stone unturned. According to the report, after ordering the destruction of the city, Scipio Aemilianus wept and behaved virtuously toward the survivors of the siege.

While Carthage lay in ruins, Utica now became the capital of Rome's African province. In 122 BCE, Gaius Sempronius Gracchus (l. 154–121 BCE), the Roman tribune, founded a small colony where Carthage used to be. This colony did not last because of Gaius's political problems and the fact that the memory of the Punic Wars still lingered. Carthage rose again five years after the death of Julius Caesar, who planned to have it rebuilt in the first instance. Soon power shifted to Carthage from

Utica since it was now the breadbasket of the Romans, owing to the agricultural fields that were still productive. Under the Romans, Carthage became a very important colony until 439 CE where it fell to the Vandals under King Gaiseric (r. 428–478 CE).

Later on, Carthage rose to prominence as Christianity grew. St. Augustine of Hippo (I. 354–430 CE) contributed to its prestige by living out life and teaching there. The Council of Carthage was held at the city because of its illustrious nature, and the Bible was as a result of the Council meeting on so many occasions so as to come up with a generally accepted and established way of life for the Western Church.

The invasion of the North by Vandals did not stop the Christianity movement there, just as the tension between the Arian Christians and Trinitarian Christians exists everywhere else.

The vandals taking advantage of their new location under the leadership of Gaiseric, plundered passing ships at will; the Romans attempted to displace them but failed, so a treaty was signed between Gaiseric and Valentinian III (r. 425–455 CE) in 442 CE. The treaty acknowledged the Vandal kingdom as a true political entity, thereby establishing peaceful relations. In 455 CE, Valentinian III was assassinated; Gaiseric disregarded the peace treaty on the account that it was between the emperor and himself. So, he set sail to Rome. He looted the city but didn't damage it or touch the populace. This was in accordance with the request from Pope Leo I (440–461). Until the death of Gaiseric, Vandals continued to profit from Carthage.

The persecution of Trinitarian Christians was reinstituted by the later Vandal King Gelimer (r. 530–534), who was an Arian Christian. His actions on the Trinitarian Christians enraged the trinitarian Roman Emperor from the East, Emperor Justinian I (r. 527–565 CE), who deployed his best general Belisarius (l. 505–565 CE) to North Africa. Belisarius, in the Vandalic War of 553–534 CE, won against Gelimer, bringing him back in chains to Constantinople, thereby restoring Carthage to the Byzantine Empire (330–1453 CE) from which she flourished.

Carthage prospered through trade under the Byzantines, providing the majority of grains for the Eastern Roman Empire. In around, 585 CE, under the Byzantine Emperor, Maurice (r. 582–602 CE), the Exarchate of Africa became Carthage. This administrative region was established separately for a more effective ruling of the Western areas of the empire.

In 698 CE, at the battle of Carthage, the Muslims defeated the Byzantine forces, driving them completely out of Africa and fully destroying the city. Subsequently, the neighboring city Tunis was fortified and developed, which became the new trade and governorship center for the region. Under the reign of the Arab Muslims, Tunis fared better than Carthage still, Carthage kept thriving until 1270 CE. This period ushered in the Eight Crusade, that is, European Crusaders took over and fortified the citadel of Byrsa. Once they were conquered, Muhammad I al-Mustansir gave the order for the city's defense to be brought down, including many of the buildings razed to the ground to prevent any further habitation.

Legacy

The conflict with the Romans is how best the world remembers Carthage, especially the Second Punic War – an event that may likely have changed the course of human history, seeing the roles the Romans played in Christianity, European history, and Western Civilization. Greek and Roman observers are often intrigued at Carthage and at the height of its power before the First Punic War, and they often pay tribute to Carthage's wealth, prosperity, and sophisticated republican governmental structure. The Punic Wars and the years following its destructions have led many to have a rethink of Carthage and all its wonders, with so many accounts of its civilization reflecting biases with propaganda shaped as a result of its numerous crises. Carthage, often portrayed for its political, cultural, and military prowess, fell to Rome, a place where "cruelty, treachery and irreligion" reigned. Now we are left with a slanted depiction of Carthage for centuries as a result of the dominant influence of the Greco-Roman perspectives in Western history.

The 20th century ushered in a more critical and well-detailed record backed by archaeological evidence across the Mediterranean, showing the civilization of Carthage to be more complex than we even anticipated. With its vast and lucrative commercial network touching every part of the ancient world, from the British Isles to Western and Central Africa and beyond, Carthaginians were enterprising and pragmatic, just like their Phoenician ancestors. They demonstrated a remarkable capacity to adapt and be innovative even when the circumstances changed, like the existential threat encountered during the Punic Wars. While art and literature might not do

Carthage any justice, there exists circumstantial evidence pointing to its multicultural and sophisticated civilization connecting people across ancient worlds, mixing their ideas, cultures, society into its own framework.

Portrayal in Fiction

Gustave Flaubert's historical novel *Salammbô* (1862) speaks of Carthage set around the time of the Mercenary War. It speaks of the boy Hannibal escaping being sacrificed; it describes in dramatic fashion child sacrifice. The film *Cabiria* by Giovanni Pastrone is narrowly based on Flaubert's novel.

The science fiction short story by Isaac Asimov called "The Dead Past," in which the main character is a historian of antiquity, is disapproving of the claims that Carthaginians carried out child sacrifices.

The boy's adventure novel by G. A. Henty titled *The Young Carthaginian* (1887) is told from Malchus's perspective about a teenage lieutenant of Hannibal during the Second Punic War.

The *Purple Quest* by Frank G. Slaughter is a fictional description of how Carthage was founded.

The Dying City is another fictional work of art that tells the story of the city of Carthage, such as the battle with the Romans and the defeat of Hannibal that came at the hand of Scipio Africanus at the great battle of Zama, written by Antonie P. Roux in Afrikaans and published in 1956.

Alternate History

The short story in Poul Anderson's *Time Patrol* series, "Delenda Est," depicts an alternate history where Hannibal won the Second Punic War, and Carthage still existed in the 20th century.

Stephen Baxter, featuring Carthage in his alternate history, *Northland* trilogy, tells of how Carthage prevails over and subjugates Rome.

John Maddox Roberts's two-part fiction, which includes *Hannibal's Children* (2002) and *The Seven Hills* (2005), is set in an alternate history where the defeat of Rome in the Second Punic War came through the hand of Hannibal and Carthage is still a major Mediterranean force to reckon with in 100 BCE.

Government

As earlier stated, the Carthaginian government was divided into a monarchy consisting of the Shophet, which was the king and the council of one hundred and four, known as the senate. Both the Shophet and the senate had the support of some segment of the population. The Shophets, for instance, had the allegiance of the military and the priests while the senate commanded the support of the merchants and that of the common people in its society. Both the Shophet and the senate were constantly after power. It was all about who held the greatest power in the kingdom, and this can be seen in the kingdom's history. At times, the king wielded more power, especially before the conflict with the Romans. But when Carthage began to lose to the Romans, political power then shifted to the hands of the council. The following list shows the Shophets according to their dynasty.

Didonids

The Didonian line consists of Dido and her direct descendants, who were of the semi-legendary founder of Carthage. Carthage prospered under their rule as a city of exploration and trade. The following are the Didonians;

Dido – 814–760 B.C.

Hanno I – 580–556 B.C.

Malchus – 556–550 B.C.

Magonids

The Magonids are of general Mago I descent, who overthrew Malchus because of his incompetence and married his (Malchus's) daughter afterward so as to draw legitimacy from the Didonian line. Carthage became a major military and colonial powerhouse under the Magonids. However, there was a fluctuation in power depending on the Shophet in power and his opposition. The Magonids include:

Mago I – 550–530 B.C.

Hasdrubal I – 530–510 B.C.

Hamilcar I – 510–480 B.C.

Hanno II – 480–440 B.C.

Himilco I – 440–406 B.C.

Mago II – 406–396 B.C.

Himlico II – 396–375 B.C.

Mago III – 375–344 B.C.

Hanno III – 344–340 B.C

Bomilcarids

Senator Bomilcar using marriage and assassination, rose to power and won himself the throne. Under the Bomilcarids' short stint in power, the island of

Sicily was conquered by the Greeks and finally lost to the Romans. The Bomilcarids include:

Bomilcar – 340–312 B.C.

Hasdrubal I – 312–274 B.C.

Gisco I – 274–240 B.C.

Barcids

The city of Carthage became orderly when Barcids came into power, unlike in the time of Bomilcarids' reign. Barcids set out to reform the economic and military structure of the land. It was during his reign that Carthage almost defeated the Romans though they ended up losing to the Romans. The Barcids include:

Hamilcar II – 240–228 B.C.

Hannibal – 228–179 B.C.

Hasdrubal II – 179–162 B.C.

Gisco II – 162–157 B.C.

Economy

At its height, the Carthaginian economy dominated the Mediterranean, even stretching across Africa to the point of maintaining many of the ancient trade routes and landmarks of its Phoenician ancestors who had also used that route during their days. Precious silks and the raw materials required to produce purple dye, which are valuable murex shells, were accessible to the Carthaginians. Carthage still retained much of its Phoenician economic legacy. Carthage also traded fish, various textiles, gold, silver, copper, tin, iron, lead, ivory, glass, wood, and other products.

Northern Africa and Hispania were the major suppliers of Carthage resources. The economy shifted as Carthage begin to lose ground to the rising Romans from solely based on trade to agriculture. During this phase, crops were used for growing the Mediterranean, with wine and grains becoming the largest agricultural export across the Mediterranean.

Agriculture

North Africa hinterland is known to be fertile, having the ability to support the growing of crops and the rearing of livestock. According to Diodorus in the 4th century BCE sharing an eyewitness account, the gardens were beautiful, with a green plantation, the estates were luxurious and large with a vast network of artificial water supply systems to give water to the land. In the mid-second century BCE, the visiting Roman envoys including Cato the

Censor described Carthage's countryside as a place where humans and animals flourish. Cato the Censor is known for his low regard as far as foreign culture is concerned, as well as his fondness for agriculture. Writing of his own experience when he visited at the same period, Polybius is of the opinion that there seemed to be a high production of livestock in Carthage as compared to other cities of the world.

Just like their Phoenician ancestors, Carthaginians didn't originally engage in agriculture. Many of the Phoenician colonies were like Carthage, located primarily along the coast, but as they settled more inland, the Carthaginians eventually took advantage of the region's rich soil developing what may have been one of the most diversified and prosperous agricultural sectors of all time – using iron ploughs, irrigation, crop rotation, threshing machines, hand-driven rotary mills, and horse mills, Carthaginians practiced productive and advanced agriculture.

Even in the face of adversity, Carthage was looking for ways to refine their agricultural techniques. Hannibal promoted agriculture after the Second Punic War to help restore Carthage's economy and to pay off the heavy war indemnity levelled on them by the Romans. The money levied on Carthage was about 10,000 talents, which equals 800,000 pounds of Roman silver, and Hannibal was very successful in paying it via agriculture. Strabo, while reporting of the years leading to the Third Punic War, noted how the devasted and improvised Carthage had made its land flourish again through agriculture. To fully understand the weight of agriculture to the Carthaginians, consider two of the retired generals known to modern-day history, Hamilcar and Mago, who made agriculture and agronomy a major part of their reign. Mago was so successful in agriculture that he had to put his knowledge in books totaling twenty-eight volumes.

These are the few materials the Romans refuse to destroy; instead, it was translated into Latin because of its rich content. Though the original copies might be lost to history, references to it from Greek and Roman writers still remain.

Circumstantial evidence pointed to the fact that before the 4th century BCE, Carthage developed viticulture and wine production. The wine produced was exported as a cigar-shaped amphora and was found in one of the archaeological sites attesting to Carthage wine production and exports.

Carthage also shipped resin wine, also known as *passum* in Latin, popular in antiquity even among the Romans. Figs, pears, and pomegranates known as "Punic apples" to the Romans were cultivated in the hinterland while olive oil was exported across the Mediterranean. Carthage also bred fine horses, which were the ancestors of today's Barb horses used for racing today and considered most influential breed after the Arabian.

Conclusion

The site that once housed the ancient city continued to be inhabited and was included as part of the Ottoman Empire in 1299–1922 CE, which was unwilling to excavate its ruins. The materials of the fallen houses, temples, and even the walls were either used for personal or administrative projects or were left where they had been found. In the 1830s CE, modern excavation began through the efforts of the Danish consulate and continued under the French between c. 1860–1900 CE.

Though further work was undertaken at the site in the first half of the 20th century, archaeologists showed more interest in the Roman history of Carthage at Sabratha and other sites. According to the cultural and political zeitgeist of that time, the Carthaginians who were Semites were defined as a people of little value, and the anti-Semitism influenced the physical evidence as well as the choice of what was kept for placement in museums or discarded.

The history of ancient Carthage still suffers not just from the city's destruction by Rome or later conflicts but from modern-day excavations also. World War II ushered in an unbiased, systematic work of ancient Carthage that serves as a template for viewing and interpreting many of the other ancient sites found. In modern-day Tunisia, Carthage still lies in ruins, which remains an important tourist and archaeological site to this day. The ruins of homes and the outlines of the great harbor can still be seen, including public baths, temples, palaces from the time when the city was the wonder of the Mediterranean as well as the jewel of the North African coast.

Chapter Five

KINGDOM OF AKSUM

The Kingdom of Aksum is also called the Aksumite Empire or even sometimes, the Kingdom of Axum; it was a kingdom that had territory spanning the northern part of Ethiopia, specifically in the region known as Tigray and also the area that is currently known as Eritrea. Men who have ruled the Kingdom of Aksum usually branded themselves with titles such as king of kings, King of Aksum, Himyar, Raydan, Salhen, Saba, Tsiyamo, and Beja of Kush. The kingdom stood for many decades, being in existence from 80 BCE to 825 CE. The kingdom's capital, where its ruler lived and exercised his administrative authority as well as discharged his duties, was located in Aksum city, and it started growing in the earliest (Iron Age) era of the kingdom's existence – particularly around the 4th century BCE and around the 1st century CE, the kingdom became well known. Sometime in history, the kingdom of Aksum grew to the point where it played a major role in the trade existing between the Empire of Rome and ancient India.

In order to make trade possible, the monarchs of the Kingdom of Aksum started to print their own money as well as laying the groundwork for their form of government, especially as the Kingdom of Kush was gradually waning at the time. From time to time, the Kingdom of Aksum started to interfere with the political issues of other kingdoms, especially those on the Arabian Peninsula, to the point that its power and authority spread vastly over that area when it conquered the Himyarite Kingdom. As at CE 274, a prophet of Manichaei known as Mani stated that Aksum was one of the greatest powers of that time alongside Rome, Persia, and China. Aksum ruled over South Arabia of Yemen for about fifty years in the 6th century.

For the purpose of religion, the people of the Kingdom of Aksum crafted monumental stelae, which they worshipped before the coming of Christianity. One of the stelae crafted by its people is today, the largest such structure in the world at ninety feet tall. It was during the reign of Ezana (fl. 320–360) that Christianity became adopted by Aksumites.

The ancient capital of the Kingdom of Aksum is also known as Aksum, and it is now a town in the Tigray Region (Northern Ethiopia). The kingdom took on the name "Ethiopia" in the 4th century. It is said that the kingdom is the place where the Ark of the Covenant was rested; further claims of their tradition also states that it was the home of the Queen of Sheba.

History

There are many theories that have been propounded about the history of Ethiopia and most of them by Carlo Conti Rossini; it was his theories that led many to believe that it was the Sabaeans whose spoken language was taken out of a Semitic branch of the major Afro-Asiatic language family that established the Kingdom of Aksum. Despite this fact, there is proof that there were Aksumites who already spoke the Semitic language, and it was these people who also adopted the Agaw people that were already speaking a different Afro-Asiatic language from the Cushitic branch of the family; furthermore, the Semitic Aksumites had already created an autonomous civilization in the Ethiopian territory before even the Sabaeans arrived.

Furthermore, more scholars discovered evidence that in such kingdoms as D'mt, there were growth and prosperity around the 10th and 15th centuries BCE, long before the Sabaeans migrated to the area in the 4th or 5th century BCE. In addition, evidence points out that the Sabaeans who settled in the area did not stay for a long time, leaving after a couple of years. All these points have thus greatly reduced the connotation that the Sabeans had anything to do with the happenings in the era at the time. Only very few settlements believe that the Sabaeans did anything in their areas, such as making up the trade group or military of one colony or another – particularly having military alliances with the D'mt civilization or an ancient state in Aksum. In the words of a scholar known as George Hatke:

> The most significant and lasting impact of these colonists was the establishment of a writing system and the introduction of Semitic speech – both of which the Ethiopians modified considerably. South Arabian culture was a foreign commodity from which the Ethiopians were able to freely pick and choose when they saw fit, rather than an entire civilization imposed by foreign rulers.

> The Ge'ez language is no longer universally thought of, as previously assumed, to be an offshoot of Sabaean or Old South Arabian, and there is some linguistic (though not written) evidence of Semitic languages being spoken in Eritrea and Ethiopia since approximately 2000 BCE. However, the Ge'ez

script later replaced Epigraphic South Arabian in the Kingdom of Aksum.

The language, Ge'ez, is not considered as derived from Sabaean or Old South Arabian any longer, unlike in previous times when it was. In fact, scholars have found proof of a spoken language in Eritrea and Ethiopia as of 2000 BCE, although the language was not written.

Empire

Aksum was a kingdom that was deeply invested in trade, and the location of the trading centers were first in Eritrea, and second, the northern part of Ethiopia. It was a kingdom that was in existence around 100–940 CE; the kingdom stemmed from the Iron Age – which was the early Aksum period – the 4th century BCE right to the year it became well-known in the 1st century CE. The first capital of the kingdom known as Mazaber was built by the son of Cush whose name was Itiyopis. Sometime later, the capital of the kingdom was moved to Axum in northern Ethiopia. The name Ethiopia was later adopted by the empire in the 4th century.

The entire territory that was owned by the Kingdom of Aksum covered the whole of contemporary Eritrea, Ethiopia, Somalia, Djibouti, and Yemen, and some areas in Sudan. The capital city that is also called by the same name, Aksum, is currently located in northern Ethiopia; however, as years have passed, the city is nothing more than a small community. Although in times past, the city was a place where all kinds of cultural and economic events were held, and it was filled with a lot of energy. There were two hills to the east side of the city, while to the west there were two streams; it is usually thought that these were the reasons why people became interested in settling in the city initially. Toward the hills and plains lying outside of the city, there are cemeteries that belong to people of Aksum and in these cemeteries are gravestones that are very detailed, and they are called stelae, or obelisks. Other major cities in the empire include Yeba, Hawulti-Melazo, Matara, Adulis, and Qohaito – among these mentioned cities, the latter three are at present in Eritrea. At the time when Endubis exercised rulership over the empire in the latter part of the 3rd century, the empire had started coining its own money; the currency was named by Mani, who said that the empire was one of the four great powers of the world at the time while the others include the Sasanian Empire, Roman Empire and "Three Kingdoms" China. Around 325 or 328 CE, the Kingdom of Aksum had adopted Christianity as the religion of the kingdom. The ruler in power at the time was King Ezana; the empire was the first to start using the picture of the cross on its coins.

Within the 3rd century, probably between c. 240, and c. 260, the people of Aksum were led to victory over the people of Sesea by *Sembrouthes*, and afterward, Sesea became a tributary of the Aksum Empire. In c. 330, King Ezana of the Kingdom of Aksum led his army into war against the Kingdom of Meroē and claimed the kingdom for himself after he conquered it. Afterward, a monument made of stone was left there, and this story is also related to Ezana Stone.

Decline

In the early 6th century, there was a second golden age, and this was followed by the waning of the Aksum Empire, which happened precisely in the middle of the 6th century, and this came to a point where the kingdom stopped minting its own coins during the early part of the 7th century. It was still during this period that the people of Aksum started to desert the capital city in a bid to go deep into the highlands believing that they would be protected there. During this time, Arab scholars still depicted Ethiopia (it was no longer called Aksum) as a state that had a vast land and was indeed powerful, even though the state no longer had control over the coasts and tributaries that were once under it. Be that as it may, whenever they lost land in the north, they found a way to gain land in the south; furthermore, Ethiopia was not a great economic power. Regardless, Arab merchants were still drawn to the state. The capital of the state was then moved; the current location is unknown, nevertheless, it was called Ku'bar or Jami.

A couple of years later, the Red Sea and Egypt were taken over in the year 646 by the Rashidun Caliphate, and this made the Aksum Empire fall into a state of isolation economically. To the northwest of Aksum, which is currently the country known as Sudan, Christian states such as Nobatia, Makuria, and Alodia survived for a long time, even until the 13th century before they converted to Islam. Although, despite being in an isolated state, the people of Aksum remained Christians.

While Degna Dian was exercising rulership over the Aksum Empire in the 10th century, Aksum continued to take over territory toward the south and even sent its army into the region that is now known as Kaffa; and at the same time, it was carrying out missionary duties in Amhara and Angot.

According to local history, a Jewish Queen by the name of Yodit (Judith) or "Gudit" overcame the kingdom and burned the churches and literature around c. 940. Scholars have found proof that there was indeed an invasion around that time period; however, many doubt that Queen Judith ever existed since they can't find any evidence that she did. However, another explanation for the invasion and eventual burning of churches was that a pagan queen by the name of Bani al-Hamwiyah of either the al-Damutah tribe or the Damoti tribe (Sidama) was responsible. Regardless of who it actually was and where she came from, modern history claims that a feminine usurper took control of the state during that time, and she ruled up until the year 1003 when her reign came to an end. Then, the empire plunged into a dark age, albeit short-lived, after which it was succeeded by the Agaw Zagwe dynasty, considerably smaller in size and landmass, in the 11th century or the 12th century (probably in 1137). The last king of Zagwe was killed by a man named Yekuno Amlak, and it was he who founded the contemporary Solomonic dynasty sometime in 1270. Yekuno Amlak discovered that he had a right to rule after he traced his ancestry to the last king of Aksum known as Dil Na'od. One thing is worth mentioning here, the fact that the Aksum Empire ended does not mean that its culture, traditions, and works of art ended as well; for instance, there is a huge influence by the empire on Zagwe dynasty architecture at Lalibela and Yemrehana Krestos Church.

Climatic Change Hypothesis

There are also some claims that the change in climatic conditions, as well as isolation in trade and economy, was what led to the decline of the Kingdom of Aksum. There was a climatic shift in the 1st century CE, which led to an increase in the local resources; more rainfall came about during spring such that it rained for six or seven months rather than the usual three and a half months. This greatly brought about an improvement in the supply of water both on the surface and subsurface, resulted in a doubling of the growing season, and created an atmosphere that could be compared to modern-day Central Ethiopia where two crops can be cultivated in a single year without the need for irrigation. This is probably the reason why the external environments of agriculture in Ethiopia were able to support the population, thus creating a very powerful commercial kingdom. It could also be the reason why no rural settlements expanded into the more fertile and productive lands of Begemder or Lasta when the kingdom was in its season of great agricultural prosperity. When profits from the international trading network dwindled, it became difficult for the kingdom to control its sources of raw materials, and that led to the eventual collapse of the trade networks.

The pressure that was already placed on the environment to provide for the kingdom's large population was further increased, and this only brought about soil erosion that started on a local scale in c. 650 and grew in magnitude by c. 700. The problem became intensified due to socioeconomic inputs, which was shown in the decline of maintenance on the land, deterioration and part desertion of land that could be cultivated, destructive exploitation of pastures, and eventually, wholesale and land degradation. All of these were brought about by a decline in rainfall between c. 730, and c. 760, the result was the reestablishment of a short growing season during the 9th century.

Foreign Relations, Trade, and Economy

The Aksum Empire was greatly involved in the trade network that existed between India and the Mediterranean (Rome, later Byzantium) since it had a territory that spanned over today's northern Ethiopia and southern and eastern Eritrea. Some of the goods being exported from Aksum included ivory, tortoise shells, gold, and emeralds, while imported goods include silk and spices. As a result of the empire's access to the Red Sea and the Upper Nile, its navy was able to acquire huge profits from trade between different states in Africa (Nubia), Arabia (Yemen), and India.

The major goods that Aksum exported were agricultural products as these were the mainstay of that period. Compared to what it is now, the land was more fertile in ancient times, and the major crops being grown were grains like wheat and barley. Livestock farming in Aksum included raising animals like cattle, sheep, and camels; Aksum people were also hunters – they hunted wild animals to obtain ivory and rhinoceros' horns. Countries with which Aksum had transactions include Rome, Egypt, and Persia. Other resources that the Kingdom of Aksum had in abundance were gold and iron – both of them were very valuable materials to trade – but there was one other item that was just as valuable, it was salt. Since the supply of salt was quite large in Aksum, it fetched the empire significant trade with other states.

The transformation of the Indian Ocean trading system in the 1st century was of huge benefit to the empire as it provided a direct link between Rome and India; in the former trade system, there was a need for voyages along the coast and various go-between ports for goods to be exported or imported. At around 100 BCE, a route was established to link Egypt and India; this called for the use of the Red Sea and using winds of the monsoon season to cross the Arabian Sea into the southern part of India. The volume of trade, and thus sea traffic, that occurred across this route grew to a huge extent, more so than was the case on older routes as of 100 CE. The sudden rise in the demand for goods from southern India by Romans led to a large number of big ships traveling down the Red Sea from Roman Egypt to the Arabian Sea and India.

The idea behind the location of the Kingdom of Aksum was so that the kingdom could be in a position where the new trade circumstances would be more favorable towards it. Not long after, Adulis turned into a port where all kinds of goods were exported, such as ivory, gold, incense, slaves, and various exotic animals. In a bid to ensure the constant supply of these goods, the kingdom's emperors made sure to develop and expand a good inland network of trade. However, as with all trading networks, there is usually a rival, and this time, it was the Kingdom of Kush, which like the Aksum Empire, worked the interior region of Africa and was the major supplier of goods to Egypt via the

River Nile. Be that as it may, the 1st century CE saw the complete takeover of the territory that previously belonged to the Kingdom of Kush by the Aksum Empire to the extent that ivory that was collected from Kush was exported through the port Adulis rather than being taken to Meroë, which was the Kush capital city. In the 2nd and 3rd century CE, Aksum went on to expand its control over the southern Red Sea basin. A wagon route to Egypt which bypassed the Nile was created. The Aksum Empire then achieved the feat of being the major supplier of African products to the empire of Rome partly because of the transformation of the Indian Ocean trading system.

Society

The people of Aksum were made up of people who spoke the Semitic language known as the Habeshas, people who spoke the Cushitic language, and people who spoke the Nilo-Saharan language such as the Kunama and Nara. Cultivation of land was performed in a reformed feudal system.

Culture

There are a couple of areas that the Aksum empire was quite famous for, and some of them include its alphabet and the Ge'ez script, which was later reformed to have vowels in it and eventually became an Abiguda. In addition, about seventeen hundred years ago, the people of the empire constructed obelisks, which were called "stelae," and these were used to mark the tombs or grave chambers of kings and noblemen of the kingdom. One of such obelisks is the most famous, known as the Obelisk of Aksum.

During the reign of King Ezana, the kingdom adopted the Christian religion in c. 325 to replace the polytheistic and Jewish religion that it was previously practicing; and this was what brought about the Ethiopian Orthodox Tewahedo Church – which gained independence from the Coptic Church in 1959 – and the Eritrean Orthodox Tewahedo Church – which received independence from the Ethiopian Orthodox church in 1993. Since the separation from the orthodox form of the church after the Council of Chalcedon in c. 451, the church became a very significant Miaphysite church; also, the scriptures and liturgy of the church still remain in Ge'ez.

Religion

The Aksum empire used to practice a polytheistic religion, which had relations with the religious practices of the southern part of Arabia before the kingdom then converted to Christianity. While they practiced the polytheistic religion, one of the items they used for worship was the crescent-and-disc symbol that was used in southern Arabia as well as the northern horn. Other sources of history claim that the pagan people of Aksum used to worship Astar, his son Mahrem and Beber.

There also exists an argument that a major change in religion came upon the Aksumites such that the only remaining old god was Astar; the other gods were substituted for a "triad of indigenous divinities" such as "Mahrem, Beber and Medr." More so, it is believed that the culture of the Aksum empire was greatly shaped by Judaism in that "the first carriers of Judaism reached Ethiopia between the reign of Queen of Sheba BCE and conversion to Christianity of King Ezana in the fourth century AC." It is further believed that "a relatively small number of texts and individuals dwelling in the cultural, economic, and political center could have had a considerable impact" and that "their influence was diffused throughout Ethiopian culture in its formative period" despite the fact that Jewish culture was greatly present and in a large magnitude. During the time when Christianity had completely found its footing in the 4th century, most of the Hebraic-

Jewish elements had already been massively accepted by the indigenes of the state and were no longer seen as foreign. In addition, they were not even thought of as posing a threat to the acceptance of the Christian religion.

Before he converted to the Christian religion, the coins, as well as inscriptions of King Ezana II, depict that he may have offered worship to the gods Astar, Medr/Meder, Beher, and Mahrem. However, there is yet another inscription that shows that Ezana was totally Christian because it made reference to "the Father, the Son, and the Holy Spirit." It was King Ezana II's teacher by the name of Frumentius who converted him to Christianity in the year 324 CE; it was also Frumentius who established the Ethiopian Orthodox Church. Frumentius was the emperor's teacher when the emperor was yet a boy, and it is believed that this set the stage for the conversion of the entire kingdom to Christianity. The evidence that points to the conversion of the empire was the replacement of the crescent and disc to the cross on their coins; be that as it may, the Jewish people of Aksum did not accept the new religion, and they created the Kingdom of Semien in rebellion. Frumentius, while having contact with the Church of Alexandria, was later appointed to be the Bishop of Ethiopia at around 330 CE.

The Church of Alexandria did not have much influence on the churches that were in Aksum, and this allowed the Aksumites to develop their own special form of Christianity. This doesn't entirely mean that there was no influence at all in the sense that, when the Church of Alexandria did not accept the Fourth Ecumenical Council of Chalcedon, churches in Aksum also backed them up, thus creating the Oriental Orthodoxy. There are certain claims that the holy relic known as the Ark of the Covenant was rested in Aksum; these claims suggest that the Ark was laid for safekeeping by Menelik I, in the Church of Our Lady Mary of Zion.

Islam entered the empire in the 7th century under the rulership of Ashama ibn-Abiar when followers of the Prophet Muhammed endured persecution from the tribe that was in power, and since the king offered them shelter, many of them migrated. In the year 622 CE, all of them went back to Medina.

Ethiopian Sources

Sources from Ethiopia, like the Nebra Nagast and the Fetha Nagast, claim that Aksum was a kingdom with Jewish culture. In the Nebra Nagast, there is a story of how the Queen of Sheba or Queen Makeda of Ethiopia met the King Solomon of Israel and a trace of Menelik I of Ethiopia, who was the son of both Queen Sheba and King Solomon. The Nebra Nagast is in itself a very old source of history (more than 700 years old), and many historians, especially those of the Ethiopian Orthodox Tewahedo Church, consider it to be a reliable source.

Coinage

Among the various states in Africa, the Kingdom of Aksum was one of the first to mint its own coins, which eventually created a legend in Ge'ez and Greece. From the time when Endubis reigned down to the reign of Armah (approx. c. 270 to c. 610), minted gold, silver, and bronze coins were already in existence. A state's ability to mint its coins was considered a huge feat in ancient periods; it meant that the Kingdom of Aksum saw itself as equal to its neighbors. Most of the coins were used to depict the events taking place whenever they were coined. For instance, the addition of a cross to the coin was used to show that the kingdom had then been converted to the Christian religion. Furthermore, with the availability of coins, it was easy for the kingdom to engage in trade, and at a certain point, proved useful when it was necessary to gather information and obtain profit.

Architecture

Generally, all the major buildings in the Kingdom of Aksum, like the palaces, for instance, were built on top of podiums that were constructed out of loose stones made to stick together with mud mortar. The corner blocks were made of granite that had been cut in little pieces, which rabbet to almost an inch at steady lengths the higher the wall was; as a result, the walls were narrower, the higher they went. The podiums upon which these buildings were constructed were usually what was left among the ruins of the Aksum Empire. The walls built upon the podiums were mostly made of loose stone placed in an alternating fashion, and these stones were usually coated with whitewash as is the case in the Yemrahana Krestos Church; there were horizontal beams that had smaller rounded beams in the stonework usually sticking out of the stone walls – referred to as "monkey heads" – on the outer side of the house and sometimes the inner side as well.

In the end, the podiums, as well as the walls, were no longer straight as they rose up; instead, there were indentations at steady lengths such that, for any wall that was high, there were areas where the stonework showed concavity and areas where they just protruded from the walls. This was done so that the walls would be much stronger. The architectural features of the houses in the kingdom such as columns, doors, windows, bases, capitals, pavings, staircases on the flank of the walls of the pavilions in the palaces, water sprouts – which mostly had the shape of a lion's head – were created out of worked granites. Doors and windows were usually made of stone or cross-members of wood, each of which was connected at the corner either by square "monkey heads" or small lintels. Some of these features were noticed in the carvings of famous stelae and rock-hewn churches of Tigray and Lalibela.

There was always a central pavilion in the palace, which usually had other substructures that were all around it; the structures also consisted of pierced doors or gates, which made sure that the occupants (kings and nobles) had some level of seclusion. The biggest structure among them all is the Ta'akha Maryam, with a measure of 390 feet in length by 260 feet in width. However, since it was discovered that the pavilion it had was smaller than those in other palaces, it was summed up that the structures of other palaces were bigger.

Certain houses made of clay serve as a representation of what small settlements used to be like in the old days. For instance, a round hut with a roof shaped in the form of a cone with layered thatches can be observed while another is a rectangular hut with the doors and windows also rectangular in shape; there are beams ending in "monkey heads" to support the roof, and then, there is the breastwork with a water spout on the roof of the house. A square-shaped house and somewhat pitch-looking thatches to serve as the roof can also be observed.

Stelae

The major part of the architectural legacy of the Kingdom of Aksum that is most easily identified are the stelae. The stelae were stone slabs used to mark graves, and they were also used to symbolize a huge and majestic palace with multiple stories. The decorations on the stelae are false doors and windows that are designed in Aksum's style of artwork. The largest one of the stelae measured 108 feet in height, if not for the fact that it broke eventually. Most of the mass of the stelae is usually kept above ground; be that as it may, they are supported by counterweights below the surface. On the stone slabs are usually engravings that have a certain pattern or design that indicates the rank of the king or the noblemen.

Chapter Six

SAHELIAN KINGDOMS

The Sahelian kingdoms were a group of centralized empires or kingdoms located on and around the Sahel – a region of land with grasslands situated in the south of the Sahara – between the 8th and 19th century. These kingdoms acquired their wealth through trade as they were in control of the trade routes that ran through the desert. The power of the kingdoms was drawn from the possession of sumpters such as camels and horses, which were fast enough to ensure that the entirety of these large empires remained under a central authority; they were also used for battles when the need arose. Although these empires were a lot less centralized, in that cities that were members of the empires enjoyed independence from the center.

The Sahelian kingdoms faced restrictions when it came to the expansion of their territories toward the south and into the forest zone of the Bono and Yoruba because warriors mounted on animals were useless in forests, and the horses, as well as camels, were not able to withstand the diseases that plagued those regions.

Economy

The Sahelian kingdoms had integrated empires that had many cities and important towns, although their territories were not very organized and their populations were rather dispersed. The people practiced agriculture, rearing of livestock, hunting, fishing, and various crafts such as metalwork, textile, and ceramics. They traveled across rivers and lakes doing trade in both short and long distances, and they had their own currencies for exchange.

History of Sahel kingdoms

Among all the Sahelian kingdoms, the Ghana Empire was the first major empire to rise in prominence. It was established in the 8th century, and it was located in what is now modern-day Senegal and Mauritania. The Ghana Empire was also the first kingdom to derive benefit from the pack animals that were introduced by Wolof traders. The period between c. 750 to c. 1078 was the period of the predominance of the Ghana Empire in the region. The smaller kingdoms during this period were Takrur, which was located west of the Ghana Empire; Malinke kingdom of Mali, which was located toward the south; and Songhai and Gao, which were located east of the empire.

After the kingdom of Ghana fell into demise, certain smaller kingdoms took over, one of which is the Sosso. By the year 1235, the Mali Empire became the most powerful nation in the region, engaging in trade with the Bono state, which was located toward the south. The Mali Empire was located on the River Niger, west of the Ghana Empire at a location now occupied by Niger and Mali; the kingdom of Mali reached the zenith of its predominance in the 1350s, however by 1400, the empire had lost the control it had over some of its feudatory states.

Among the Sahelian kingdoms, the most powerful was the Songhai Empire, which expanded its territories quickly starting during the reign of King Sonni Ali in the 1460s. By the year 1500, the empire had land stretching from Cameroon to the Maghreb and was the largest kingdom in the history of Africa. However, the empire did not stand for long as in 1951, the empire crumbled due to the fact that it was attacked by a Moroccan army unit (musketeers).

Deep into the east, on the Lake Chad, rose another very powerful empire known as Kanem-Bornu, although when it was founded in the 9th century, it was only known as Kanem. To the west of Kanem were the barely united Hausa city-states that also became predominant. Both of these kingdoms had an anxious coexistence between them; however, they both were stable.

With the coming of the year 1810, the rising of the Fulani Empire came about after it had conquered the Hausa, it then created an empire that was more centralized. Both the Fulani Empire and the Kanem-Bornu continued to coexist.

Sahelian Kingdoms
Kingdom of Alodia
Alodia was a kingdom located in the region of modern-day central and southern Sudan. The capital of the kingdom was Soba, which is located in what is now Khartoum at the point of convergence between the Blue and White Nile Rivers. The kingdom met its demise in 350 CE.

Bamana Empire
The Bamana Empire was a Sahelian kingdom that was located at Ségou, which is now a part of Mali. It was founded after the great Mali Empire and the Keita dynasty waned. The empire had a strong economy because trading with other nations boomed. The Kulubali or Coulibaly dynasty ruled the kingdom.

Kingdom of Baol

The Baol Kingdom was one of the kingdoms to rise out of the division that the Wolof Empire faced in the year 1555. The capital of the city was Diourbel, and that was the dwelling place of the kingdom's ruler, Teigne. The territory that the kingdom possessed spanned from the ocean to the capital city, and some of the towns include Touba and Mbacke. The Kingdom of Baol was located toward the south of the Cavor Kingdom, and from the Kingdom of Sine, it was located toward the north.

Kanem-Bornu Empire

The area of land which was occupied by Kanem-Bornu is what is now present-day Chad and Nigeria. It was once famed the Kanem Empire to Arabic geographers during the 8th century CE, and it became the Independent Kingdom of Bornu or (Bornu Empire) until 1900. The Kanem Empire (which was what it was known as between c. 700 to c. 1380) spanned over modern-day Chad, Nigeria, and Libya. At the pinnacle of its existence, the Kanem Empire covered the majority of Chad, a portion of southern Libya (Fezzan), Eastern Niger, northeastern Nigeria, and the northern part of Cameroon. The Bornu Empire, which lasted between the 1380s to 1893, at some point became larger in terms of territory than Kanem in that it spanned over a portion of Chad, Niger, Sudan, and Cameroon; although as of today, the empire is now in the northeastern part of Nigeria.

Daju

Oral traditions have it that the Daju are a people who arrived in Darfur from either the east or the south, probably the region of Shendi in Nubia. The language of the Daju people sounds a lot like that of the Nobim. They established a kingdom in southern Jebel Marra, and from that location, they exerted their influence and power over the neighboring states in regions that were located toward the south and south-east. According to the Arab historian al-Idrisi, the Daju people were camel breeders.

Funj Sultanate

The Funj Sultanate was a kingdom whose territory spanned across present-day Sudan, the northwestern part of Eritrea, and the western part of Ethiopia. The kingdom was established in the year 1504 by the Funj people; Islam was the religion of the kingdom. The pinnacle of the kingdom's existence was the 17th century; however, that height was short-lived because, in the 18th century, the kingdom declined and finally crumbled.

Ghana Empire

The Ghana Empire existed from c. 300 up to c. 1100, and the proper name for the empire was Wagadou – this was also the name of its ruler. It was a kingdom that was located in West Africa in a place that is now currently southeastern Mauritania and western Mali. There were a lot of states in the region that engaged in the trans-Saharan trade selling gold and salt in ancient times; however, when camels were introduced into the western Sahara in the 3rd century, it brought about major changes in the region, which then resulted in the Ghana Empire. During the period where Islam conquered all of North Africa in the 7th century, the use of camels had paved way for the emergence of unusual trade routes and as well as a trade network that ran from Morocco to the Niger River. This trans-Saharan trade of both salt and gold made the Ghana Empire very rich; afterward, bigger and better urban centers started developing. The increase in trade volumes also brought about expansion in territory, in a bid to secure control over other trade routes.

The actual emergence of the dynastic rulership of the Ghana Empire is not known; written history only mentions it in the year 830 by Muhammad ibn Mūsā al-Khwārizmī. A scholar by the name of al-Bakri from Cordoba traveled to the area in the 11th century and then recorded in detail a description of the empire.

During the empire's decline in the 13th century, it became a liege subject of the Mali Empire, which was rising at the time. When the Gold Coast became the first nation in sub-Saharan Africa to gain its independence from colonial powers, it renamed itself Ghana as a way to honor the empire that had been lost.

Origin

The earliest discourses regarding the origin of the Ghana Empire can be found in the Sudanese chronicles of Mahmud Kati and Abd al-Rahman al-Saadi. Kati's work depicts that twenty kings ruled Ghana before the coming of the Prophet, and the empire even lasted over a century after the Prophet. According to him, the rulers of the empire came from one of the three following origins: Soninke, Wangara (this is a Soninke group), and Sanhaja Berbers.

The 16th-century interpretations of the genealogies of kings of the empire linked Ghana to the Sanhaja original interpretations; al-Idrisi, an 11th-century writer, and ibn Said, a 13th-century writer, both believed that the rulers of the Ghana Empire drew their ancestry from a clan of the Prophet Muhammed either through Ali, his son-in-law or Abi Talib, his protector. According to ibn Said, twenty-two kings reigned over the empire before the Hijra, and afterward, twenty-two others reigned. Although these early views give a certain unusual interpretation of the origin of Wagadou, they are most often not well regarded by scholars. For instance, al-Idrisi's view is not well regarded because his work shows that there were glaring miscalculations in geography and historical chronology; on the other hand, al-Kati's and al-Saadi's view is argued to have stemmed from nomads who trespassed the territory after the demise of the empire, mistaken to be members of the original population. Furthermore, it is argued that al-Kati and al-Saadi totally ignored or did not give enough amount of consideration to the accounts of modern-day writers who all report that the population and rulers of the Ghana Empire to be "negroes."

History of Islam in the Ghana Empire

Contemporary scholars have since time past had a long and lasting controversy about how vast the empire of Ghana was and how long the kingdom stood. Islam was a religion that was very prominent in the Asian-African-European region. According to Abu-Abdullah Adelabu, who is an African Arabist, non-Islamic authorities on history do not regard the significance of how the territory of the Ghana Empire expanded because they do not want to acknowledge the fact that Islam had a serious influence on the empire. In one of his books, the scholar states that Muslim historians and geographers in Europe such as Abu-Ubavd al-Bakri from Cordoba have had their works suppressed in order for opposing views of non-Islamic Europeans to be held. He noted the refusal of the non-Muslim Europeans to recognize Ibn Yasin's *Geography of School Of Imam Malik* that contained a detailed account of activities in the Ghana Empire, both social and religious, which have established concrete evidence of a bias in the composition of documentations of the empire's history by European historians especially because they relate to Islam and Muslim societies in ancient times. In the words of Adelabu:

The early Muslim documentaries including Ibn Yasin's revelations on ancient African major centers of Muslim culture crossing the Maghreb and the Sahel to Timbuktu and downward to Bonoman had not just presented researchers in the field of African History with solutions to how scarce written sources were in large parts of sub-Saharan Africa, it even consolidated confidence in techniques of oral history, historical linguistics and archaeology for authentic Islamic traditions in Africa.

Oral Traditions

During the latter part of the 19th century, colonial officers started to collect accounts of the tradition of the ancient Ghana Empire, and some of those accounts include manuscripts that were written in Arabic; it was during this time that French troops occupied the region. Most of these traditions were not only recorded but also published. The traditions stated that the empire was established by a man whose name was Dinga, who emerged "from the east" and continually migrated to a number of various places in western Sudan; and for each place he settled, he left children after having a wife there. In a bid to acquire power at the final place he settled, he had to slay a goblin and then become married to his daughters, who eventually became the ancestors of clans that had more influence and control in the region at the time. After the death of Dinga, Khine and Dyabe, who were both his sons had a contest for the empire's rulership; Dyabe won the contest, and thus, the kingdom was founded.

Koumbi Saleh

Koumbi Saleh, which is on the border of the Sahara Desert, is believed to be the place where the capital of the Ghana Empire stood. According to the way in which al-Bakri describes it, the capital was actually two towns that were separated by "continuous habitations" of about six miles such that they were sometimes thought of as being merged to become one.

El-Ghaba

The major part of the city in the ancient Ghana Empire was El-Ghaba and that was where the king resided. With a stone wall to protect it, it played the function of being both the royal and spiritual capital of the kingdom. There lay in the city, a sacred grove where priests resided as well as the palace of the king, which also happened to be the largest building in the city and it was surrounded by other "domed buildings." Also, in the city, lay a single mosque for when Muslim officials came visiting.

Muslim District

No record of the name of the second part of the city exists; however, wells having fresh water in them surrounded it because that was where vegetables were cultivated. Most of its inhabitants were Muslims; there were twelve mosques, one of these mosques was built primarily for Friday prayers, and it had a complete group of scribes, scholars, and legal experts. Most of the Muslims in this part of the city were merchandisers; this is why some think that it was the principal business district. It is very probable that the merchants were black Muslims referred to as the Wangara or, as they are called in the modern day, Dyula and Jakhanke. The practice of running towns or cities that are autonomous of the influence of the main government is something that can only be attributed to the Dyula and Jakhanke Muslims in all of history.

Economy

The majority of the knowledge that pertains to the economy of the ancient Ghana Empire was obtained from al-Bakri. According to him, all the businessmen were mandated to pay a tax of one gold dinar on all sports importations, and for export, they had to pay two gold dinars. As for other commodities, the dues were fixed, and this included copper. Most of the imported goods were likely textile materials, ornaments, and other products. The designs of many of the leather goods that were handcrafted and found in Morocco were traced to the empire. Koumbi Saleh, the empire's capital, was the major center for trade. The ownership of all the solid gold in the empire was claimed by the king, leaving only gold dust to the people. The influence of the king was exercised upon local regions; as a result, the different chiefdoms and tributary states had to pay tributes to the outer boundary of the empire.

When camels were introduced into the trading system, it paved the way for the success of the Soninke in that goods could be transported in a more efficient manner over the Sahara. All of these factors helped the empire to remain a powerful state for some time, bringing about an economy that was not only stable but also wealthy, thereby facilitating its survival for centuries. The empire was also very well known for being a hub for education.

Decline

Considering that the sources from which the story of ancient Ghana was gathered are scattered in nature, there is no way to determine the exact period of the decline of the empire. The quondam sources that describe the empire are unclear; however, as al-Bakri noted, the kingdom had forced Awdaghost in the desert under its rule between years 970 and 1054. At the time of al-Bakri, the empire was already bordered by powerful kingdoms like Sila, and by the year 1240, the kingdom had already become a part of the Mali Empire, thus establishing its end.

According to a tradition in historiography, the demise of the Ghana Empire was brought about by its pillaging under the hands of the Almoravid movement, which took place in 1076 and 1077 in spite of the resistance that the Ghanaians posed towards the attack for approximately ten years. However, this tradition was disregarded by Conrad and Fisher (1982), who are of the opinion that the attack launched by the Almoravid troops was nothing but a myth that was derived from misinterpretation or unenlightened dependence on Arab sources. Although there are some scholars who disagree with the arguments of Conrad and Fisher, the fact remains that there is no archaeological proof that the Ghana Empire underwent any radical change, neither is the decline of the empire in any way linked to the era of conquests of the Almoravid army.

Notwithstanding the unclear evidence that the Ghana Empire was conquered, sources of the empire's history give an account of the nation's conversion to Islam as documented by al-Idrisi, who wrote down the information he gathered in the year 1154, and at the time, the entire state was already Muslim. A North African authority in history by the name of Ibn Khaldun, who referenced the work of both al-Bakri and al-Idrisi, stated that the power of the Ghana Empire started to dwindle as the power of the "veiled people" began to rise, via the Almoravid movement. The report that was given by al-Idrisi did not provide grounds that the empire was facing demise or that its power was weakening at the time he published the report, which was seventy-five years after al-Bakri had already published his own account; instead, al-Idrisi described the capital of the empire saying it was "the greatest of all towns of the Sudan with respect to area, the most populous, and with the most extensive trade." The only clear information was the account of al-Umari in the year 1340, which recorded that the Ghana Empire was adopted into the empire of Mali. After it was incorporated into the Mali Empire, Ghana remained a kind of kingdom with its ruler being the only person permitted to bear the name Malik and was "like a deputy" to the Mali emperor.

Aftermath and Sosso Occupation

Ibn Khaldun recorded that after the Ghana Empire converted to Islam, "the authority of the rulers of Ghana dwindled away and they were overcome by the Sosso [...] who subjugated and subdued them." Later traditions believe that from the late 19th century to the 20th century, Diara Kante assumed leadership of the Koumbi Saleh, and afterward, he founded the Diarisso Dynasty. Soumaoro Kante, son of Diara Kante assumed rulership after his father and forced the citizens to pay tributes to him. The Sosso also took over the territory of its neighbor to the south, the Mandinka state of Kangaba, in which the major goldfields of Bure were sited.

Malinke Rule

In the brief record given by ibn Khaldun regarding the history of Sudan, he noted, "The people of Mali outnumbered the peoples of the Sudan in the neighborhood and dominated the whole region." He continued saying that Mali "vanquished the Sosso and acquired all their possessions, both their ancient

145

kingdom and that of Ghana." Modern tradition has it that Sundiata Keita was the leader of the Mali revivification (Sundiata Keita was the man who established the Mali Empire and was the swayer of its core region, Kangaba). The tradition further notes that Ghana, who was then a feudatory of the Sosso, decided to hoist a rebellion against Kangaba, after which it became a member of a group of Mande-speaking lands. After Soumaoro was defeated at the Battle of Kirina (1235, an arbitrary year assigned by Delafosse), the new swayers of Koumbi Saleh became complete allies with the Empire of Mali. With the accompaniment of Mali's growth in power, the role of Koumbi Saleh as an ally was reduced to that of a mere subservient land.

Empire of Great Fulo

The Empire of Great Fulo, or as it was also called, the Denanke Kingdom, was a Pulaar kingdom of Senegal that existed before the coming of Islam. The kingdom was in control of the Futa Tooro area, and it exercised dominance and influence over the neighboring kingdoms via the use of its military as well as through the wars it fought with the empires of Mali and Songhai.

Jolof Empire

The Jolof Empire or the Wolof Empire was a kingdom that was based in what is now the nation of Senegal. For almost two centuries, the rulers of this kingdom received tributes from its liege states, who agreed to become liege states without being forced. The kingdom's demise stemmed from the defeat of the Buurba Jolof by the lord of Kavor at the Battle of Danki.

Kaabu Empire

The Kaabu Empire was a large empire that was located in the region of Senegambia and had territory spanning what is today the northeastern part of Guinea-Bissau, the majority of present-day Gambia, and down to Koussanar, Koumpentoum, parts of southeastern Senegal, and Casamance in Senegal. The kingdom was once an imperial army state of the Mali Empire.

Kingdom of Kano

The Kingdom of Kano was a Hausa kingdom that existed before 1000 CE in the north of present-day northern Nigeria. It stood for a long time until it was proclaimed the Sultanate of Kano.

Mali Empire

The Mali Empire was established by Sundiata Keita; it existed between 1235 to 1670. The Mali Empire started as a small state of Mandinka in the upper regions of River Niger. It was between the 11th and 12th centuries that it evolved into an empire after the decline and fall of the Ghana Empire. In 1670, Bamana invaded and burned down Niani, and not long after, the Mali Empire fell.

Mossi Kingdoms

The Mossi kingdoms were a group of powerful nations in present-day Burkina Faso that had control over the Upper Volta River for many centuries. These kingdoms were established as a result of the marriage of warriors from the Mamprusi area of today's Ghana with the women in the region.

Kingdom of Saloum

The Kingdom of Saloum was a Serer/Jolof kingdom based in what is today's Senegal. The rulers of the kingdom probably originated from Mandinka/Kaabu. The capital city of the state was Kahone, and it was a sister kingdom to Sine. The history, culture, and geography of both kingdoms were connected such that they were referred to as Sine-Saloum.

Shilluk Kingdom

The location of the Shilluk Kingdom was along the White Nile River bank in today's South Sudan. The capital of the city, which was the ruler's residence, was Fashoda. Folk history has it that the kingdom was founded by its first ruler, who was a demigod by the name of Nyikang.

Kingdom of Sine

The Kingdom of Sine was a Serer kingdom that was located on the bank to the north of the Saloum River delta in present-day Senegal. Inhabitants of the kingdom were known as *Siin-Siin* or *Sine-Sine*.

Sokoto Caliphate

Sokoto Caliphate was an autonomous Sunni Muslim caliphate that was established during the jihad war of 1804 by Usman Dan Fodio in West Africa. At the pinnacle of its existence, this kingdom connected more than thirty emirates and more than ten million people into one kingdom. It was among the most important empires in 19th century Africa.

Songhai Empire

The Songhai Empire was a kingdom that exercised dominance of the western Sahel during the 15th and 16th centuries. During the time the kingdom was at its pinnacle, it was among the largest empires in the history of Africa. The empire was forced to go down when plots and coups were used to ascend the throne during the reign of the Askia dynasty.

Sultanate of Darfur

The Sultanate of Darfur was a kingdom before the colonial era in what is now Sudan. It existed between the year 1603 and October 24, 1874 at which time it fell into the hands of Rabih az-Zubayr who was a warlord from Sudan. At the height of its existence, which was the late 18th to early 19th century, the kingdom spanned over Darfur down to Kordofan and the western banks of the White Nile; thus, it attained territory as large as modern-day Nigeria.

Pashalik of Timbuktu

The Pashalik of Timbuktu was established in 1591 when military troops of about three or four thousand soldiers plus auxiliaries from Morocco left Marrakesh, overcame the Songhai army at Tondibi, and subdued Gao, Timbuktu, and Dienné. Timbuktu was made the capital. In 1787, the Tuareg subdued Timbuktu, and Pashalik was made into a tributary.

Tunjur Kingdom

There are no records of how the Tunjur kingdom was established; however, it is known that the kingdom substituted a previous Daju kingdom. The lands under the control of the Tunjur kingdom spanned across modern Sudan and even up to present-day Chad. In the early 16th century, it ruled over Darfur and Wadai.

Wadai Sultanate

The Wadai Sultanate was a sultanate in Africa that was located toward the east of Lake Chad in modern-day Chad and the Central African Republic. It was during the reign of the first sultan, Abd al-Karim, that the kingdom emerged in the 17th century after subverting the Tunjur people in the area.

Wassoulou Empire

The Wassoulou Empire, also referred to as the Mandinka Empire, was an empire in West Africa whose establishment was built upon the conquests of Malinke ruler, Samori Ture. The empire did not stand for long, existing only between 1878 and 1898.

Chapter Seven

MALI EMPIRE

The Mali Empire flourished as a trading empire in western Africa from the 13th to 16th century; it is known as one of the largest empires in the history of West Africa. At its peak, the Mali Empire stretched from the Atlantic coast to parts of the Sahara Desert (central areas). From historical studies, the Mali Empire was birthed in 1235 CE and thrived until the 1600s CE. The rise of the empire was preceded by the short-lived Sosso Kingdom ruled by Sumanguru Kante. The Sosso King successfully conquered several Malinke kingdoms that were part of the ancient Ghana empire (which is not related to present-day Ghana) located around the upper Niger River in the early 13th century. Before their conquest, the Malinke, including those in Kanganba, were middlemen in trades, especially the gold trade.

The Sosso king or chief (as he is sometimes referred to) became infamous due to his harsh, oppressive, and ineffective rules. This provoked the revolt by the Malinke resistance under the leadership of Sundiata in 1230 CE. Sundiata is believed to be the brother of Kanganba's fugitive ruler. In 1235 Sundiata and his army defeated the king of Sosso, Sumanguru Kante. Many historians, including the likes of Innes Gordon and Conrad David, believe 1235 was the birth year of the great Mali Empire, whose history is still being discussed in oral traditions. The birthplace of Sundiata Niani became the capital of the empire, and from there, he extended through the Atlantic Coast located south of the Senegal River all through to Gao, located east of the Niger bend.

King Sundiata deployed imperial armies to subdue the lands to the south of Bambuk and Bondu. These territories were known as "gold-bearing land." To the northeast, Diara was overcome, and the imperial armies continued north along the Niger to Lac Debo, still under the rule of King Sundiata. While under Mansa Musa, the Mali Empire rose to its greatest height. Mali conquered the famous trading cities of Gao and Timbuktu. Mansa Musa also took over the towns Taghaza and Walata that were very rich in salt deposits to the north and south Sahara, respectively. The Mali Empire extended its rule over its eastern borders to include the Hausa people. The peoples of Tukulor and Fulani, including Takrur, were conquered to the western borders. In places like Egypt and Morocco, ambassadors and imperial agents were sent to represent the emperor.

Administration

Sundiata laid the foundation for the administration that every other emperor would build upon. All through the history of the Mali Empire, the king, also referred to as mansa, was assisted by an assembly of local chiefs or elders. This assembly, headed by the mansa, held meetings either indoors in the palace or outdoors under a tree in the presence of the audience. The mansa had supreme or absolute powers over the judicial system, and he acted as the only source of justice. The mansa never had legal advisors but he had ministers that helped in in the day to day running of the empire. Some of these ministers include the master of the treasury (this was formerly called granaries), the chief of the army, the royal orchestra leader, and the master of ceremonies. Although the king had these ministers, he was supreme and had monopoly power over important trades. Some of the trades the king had a monopoly over include; gold nuggets. All other traders had to deal in gold dust.

The king was believed to have magical powers, which caused his citizens to be loyal to him and his slaves exclusively loyal. Whenever the king ate, no one was permitted to be in his presence, and all visitors had to come before the king barefoot, bow down and sprinkle dust on their heads before coming to him. The king's leadership was like that of a cult and could not be questioned or debated. This resulted in a highly centralized system of government. The fate and fortune of the empire depended solely on the king. If the king was talented (like Mansa Musa), the empire would progress, and if it lacked talent, the empire would suffer. Under Sundiata, the empire progressed and incorporated Walata, the old kingdoms of Ghana, Songhai, and Tadmekka. Niani, which was located around the Sankarani River, was chosen to be the capital of the empire.

Apart from the fact that Niani was the birthplace of Sundiata, Niani was chosen because of its strategic location. Niani was surrounded by mountains, which gave it a military advantage. Another strategic advantage of Niani was that it was very close to major areas like waterways and forests, which acted as sources to trade goods (such as salt and gold).

After conquering a place, local chiefs who were loyal were left to continue ruling their people while the disloyal ones were replaced by someone else from the chiefdom who was loyal. To ensure that local chiefs remained loyal, they were assisted by a governor appointed by the emperor. The governors had control over a garrison stationed in the conquered territories.

The Mali Empire ensured continued loyalty by taking members of the royal class as hostages and remanding them in Niani, the capital. Every chiefdom was expected to pay tributes to the emperor, and the appointed governors oversaw this. The Mali Empire had a very functional administrative system, which was the reason it flourished and attained the height of the wealthiest empire in Africa's history. The Mali Empire's wealth astonished both Arabia and Europe. Visitors from Europe and Arabia were also astounded by the high level of justice they noticed in its society. They also experienced an uncommon level of security and safety, as visitors could move around freely and conduct trade without fear of being attacked. In all villages of the empire, food was in abundance.

Military

The Mali Empire developed a highly trained and powerful military. This is heavily reflected in the frequency and number of its military conquest beginning from the late 13th century and all through the 14th century. The initial organization of the military is credited to Sundiata. Although subsequent emperors inherited a very functional military, the empire's military underwent a series of important changes before it could attain its legendary status that was the envy of all. These steady and radical changes were made possible by two things: the first was the steady influx of taxes, which was used to service the military and equip them with the most sophisticated weapons; the second was the stability and continuity in government that began in the concluding part of the 13th century all through to the 14th century. These reasons were also behind the advancement of the empire's power within and beyond its boundaries. The empire's army was highly organized and had a special elite corps of horsemen. It also had numerous foot soldiers in every battalion. The military was charged with the responsibility of protecting the empire's flourishing trade by defending its borders from external and internal attacks.

The weapons used by the army were largely dependent on the region of origin of the troop. And because the empire was vast, it would be accurate to say that the empire's army made use of several kinds of weapons. Among all its troops, the sofa were the only ones directly equipped by the capital, and they heavily made use of bows and arrows (poisoned). The Mandekalu troops from the north were equipped with shields made of animal hide and short spears for stabbing, known as tamba. Warriors from the south were also armed with bows and poisoned arrows. The bow was a prominent symbol in the Mali Empire's warfare as it was used to symbolize military force. The garrison and field armies were largely made up of bowmen. In fact, in Kaabu, the troops had a ratio of three bowmen to one spearman. The bowmen made use of arrows that were iron-tipped and mostly poisoned. In addition, bowmen were equipped with a knife and two quivers that were tied behind their arms. For siege warfare, the empire's army made use of flaming arrows. The infantry was equipped with bows and spears and the cavalry was equipped with foreign and locally made lances and swords. The imperial army also had as one of its weapons, poisoned javelins that were heavily used in skirmishes. Horsemen wore helmets made of iron, mail armor for their defense, and carried shields that were similar to those carried by the infantry.

The empire mandated every clan to provide a quota of fighting-age men whenever the emperor demanded. These men were freemen known as the Horon caste, and they were expected to come with their own weapons. That way, the empire maintained a quasi-professional full-time army always on standby to defend or advance its borders. Historians record the empire's army's peak to be one hundred thousand, with cavalry making up ten thousand. The armies could be deployed on short notice throughout the empire with the help of the water clan. There are numerous historical sources that affirm that war canoes and other vessels for war transport were used frequently in the inland waterways of West Africa. Most of these canoes were constructed using single logs or carved out from a big tree trunk.

The imperial armies were later divided into two divisions, known as the southern and northern commands. These commands were under the command of the sankar-zouma and farim-soura, respectively. These leaders were both members of the emperor soldier elites that were referred to as "ton-ta-jon-ta-ni-woro." The ton-ta-jon-ta-ni-woro was a squad of sixteen slaves who carried quivers. These warrior elites had a representative known as ton-tigi (quiver master). At the Gbara, each of the ton-tigi was charged with providing counsel to the mansa or emperor, but among the ton-tigi, sankar-zouma and farim-soura had more powers, and it is even believed that all other ton-tigi were under them.

These ton-tigi were members of a special force that was made up of cavalry commanders known as "brave men" (translated from farari). These commanders had a team of individual farariya or "braves" under their command. Each farariya was made up of some infantry captains or officers referred to as duukunasi or kele-koun. In battle, the duukunasi or lele-koun were responsible for leading troops under the command of a "brave man" (farimba) or a "great brave man" (farima), respectively. Apart from their commandant, another slight difference is that unlike the kele-koun who led freemen, the duukunasi led sofa, a slave troop responsible for guarding the horses. The farimba carried out their duties from the garrison under the protection of the entire slave troops. While on the other hand, the farima carried out its operations on the battlefield with all freemen.

Economy

Just like the Sosso Kingdom and the ancient Ghana Empire before it, the Mali Empire flourished for two major reasons; strategic location and trade. The empire was located between the rain forest in the southern part of West Africa and the Islamic caliphate in the northern part of Africa. The empire's interior was readily accessible through the route provided by the Niger River to the Atlantic Coast. While from the north, the empire traded goods, and this was made possible by the Berber-controlled camel caravans, which crossed the Sahara Desert. As mentioned earlier, the Mali Empire had three main sources of revenue, which were acting as middlemen by buying goods and selling at a much higher price, taxes for passage of goods, and access to valuable natural resources. Among these natural resources were gold found in the regions of Bambuk, Galam, and Bure under the sovereign rule of the empire. With the control of the resources, the empire had a rich foreign exchange. Gold dust was exchanged for salt in the Sahara. As the development of minting coinage in precious metals progressed in places such as Italy (precisely Genoa and Venice) and Spain (Castile), gold was in high demand.

Another trading opportunity was opened to the Mali Empire in the wake of the 14th century. This opportunity came as a result of the conquest and incorporation of territories in the inland Delta, such as the eastern Songhai and Gao. These provinces contributed greatly to resources from farming, hunting, fishing, and grazing. Also, these new provinces were sources of slaves for the military, slaves for trade, and slaves for production. Also, the empire's treasury felt the impact of the addition of these two new provinces as tributes from their chiefs and kings were paid to the empire to pledge their loyalty. The conquest of these provinces also meant the control of new trade routes, which translated into the payment of tariffs to the empire. When

Mansa Musa ascended the throne in the mid-14th century, he embarked on numerous pilgrims to Cairo. On his trips, he was extravagant in his spending and gifting, and this publicized not only his wealth but the wealth of the empire throughout North Africa, the Middle East, as well as Europe. The stories that were told about the empire's wealth attracted many traders to the Sahara. In fact, there are historic documentations that Egyptian traders were frequent visitors to the Mali Empire. One such evidence was the Malians in Walata, which was a commercial center, wearing imported clothes from Egypt. This outcome is believed to have been the result of Mansa Musa's pilgrimage. The Mali Empire also extended its trade to the Maghreb region. This was achieved under Mansa Musa, who exchanged embassies with the sultan of Morocco. Among the commodities that were traded in the trans-Saharan trade route were salt, slaves, ivory, animal hides, copper, and gold (which was the most prestigious commodity). European, North African, and Middle Eastern monarchs competed for gold in the trans-Saharan trade, which the Mali Empire had control over and dominated.

The conquest and incorporation of the trade center Timbuktu also boosted the economy of the empire. Timbuktu was founded by the Tuaregs (nomads) in the 12th century. Under the nomadic Tuaregs, Timbuktu acted as a quasi-independent trade port. The port had two advantages: one was that it was located in the Niger River bend, and two, it was where the trans-Saharan caravan started from. When the Mali Empire took over Timbuktu, they upgraded to be one of the most cosmopolitan and important trade centers in the history of Africa. Important and luxurious goods such as weapons, textile, kola nuts, ivory, glassware, sugar, sorghum, spices, millet, craft products, military, transportation horses, and slaves were traded in Timbuktu. In some instances, goods were exchanged with other goods (trade by barter). While other times, goods were paid for using the generally or personally acceptable currency, which could either be gold ingots or copper, an agreed quantity of ivory or salt, or cowry shells obtained from Persia.

Rulers

Ibn Khaldun and Abu Abdullah Muhammed ibn Battuta are among the three historians (and geographers) who equipped the followers of history with detailed documentation of the Mali Empire during the medieval era. Some of these scholars documented the power and greatness of the Mali Empire to be second to none throughout the history of Western Sudan. Sundiata or Sunjata became king after successfully revolting and defeating the Sosso or Sosso kingdom. He is believed to be the greatest Mali king ever. According to records, he ruled for about twenty-five years. Mansa Wali, his son, succeeded him, and he as well, according to historical beliefs, was a great king. Mansa Wali was renowned mostly for his pilgrims to Mecca from around 1260 to 1277, which was during the period Sultan Baybars reigned. Like most African kingdoms or empires, the Mali Empire went through a series of leadership tussles. And unlike most, she endured and was able to reach her peak. Mansa Wati, who was a brother to Mansa Wali, succeeded him, although Mansa Wati had nothing special documented about him. Mansa Wati was succeeded by Mansa Khalifa, who was another brother to Mansa Wali. Mansa Khalifa had special attributes that he is remembered for. But all were negative. Mansa Khalifa was believed to be an insane king who had no respect for the life of his citizens. In fact, he would use them as targets for archery practices. Mansa Khalifa was assassinated by his own people, who grew tired of his insanity. He was succeeded by Mansa Abu Bakr. Mansa Abu Bakr's mother was a sister to the three mansas that preceded him, which means she was a daughter to Sundiata. It is a common belief among historians that the problem of the empire began from about this time, as would be proven by the next mansa.

Mansa Abu Bakr was succeeded by Mansa Sakura, who was not a member of the royal family. He was a military commander who is believed to have had the support of the majority due to the ineffectiveness of the royal family. He also made pilgrims to Mecca, a journey that took months from Mali. Historians draw their conclusion of Mansa Sakura having the support of the people from his journey to Mecca; they believed that there was no way he could have afforded to be away from the empire for that long if he wasn't popular among the people. Sakura is known to be one of the greatest kings of the empire as he stabilized the empire politically. This had a positive effect on trade, thus increasing the empire's prosperity. Mansa Sakura is also credited with the expansion of the eastern borders to include the territory of Songhai. Many believe Gao was conquered during his reign as well. Mansa Sakura was killed in one of his pilgrimage to Mecca. After his death, the kingship reverted to the royal family and precisely to descendants of Sundiata. Two successive descendants of Sundiata ruled with no records worthy of note. They were succeeded by a descendant of Mansa Sundiata's brother, whose name was Manden Bori. He was a Muslim and had Abu Bakr as his Arabic name.

Mansa Musa I

Mansa Musa was a descendant of Maden Bori, and he is believed to have brought the empire back to its golden age after years of failed leadership. Mansa Musa established an imperial army of about one hundred thousand men, among which ten thousand of those men were armored cavalry corps with horses. He had Saran Mandian, who was very skillful in the act of warfare as his general. With this force, Mansa Musa could not only enforce his rule within his territory, but he would also go ahead to extending the empire's frontier. Historians believe that under the rule of Mansa Musa, the territories of the Mali Empire were doubled. He extended and enforced the empire's rule on all sides of its borders; to the east, he re-enforced the empire's control of Gao that was located along the Niger River. To the west, he extended his rule to the lower parts of Senegal and Gambia. The forest situated in what came to be referred to as the Gold Coast and the region of Bure were conquered and controlled by the empire to the south. To the north, which is along the western Sahara, every tribe was subdued, and as the empire grew, so too did the religious, linguistic, and ethnic features.

Under the administration of Mansa Musa, detailed records were kept, and copies were sent to the central office located in Niani, which was the capital. Mansa Musa ruled the empire and its diverse people by personally appointing governors known as farba. These governors were in charge of allocated provinces. They were to collect taxes, peacefully settle disputes, including tribal, and provide justice in their provinces. Under Mansa Musa, the empire prospered greatly because tributes were coming to the capital from trades, tributes from conquered chiefs, sales of natural resources. The empire had so much wealth that the king single-handedly crashed the price of bullion by 20 percent by giving away so much gold on his visit to Cairo in 1324 CE. This resulted in the rumor that spread as far as Spain in c. 1375 that the streets of Mali were littered with gold. In fact, in the first-ever European detailed map of West Africa, the land of Mali was branded as a huge reserve of gold, with Mansa Musa wearing an enormous crown made of gold. These rumors have a lot to play in kindling the interests the Europeans later developed in West Africa and Timbuktu, the great trading city.

Mansa Sulayman

Mansa Musa was succeeded by his son Mansa Magha in 1337. But Mansa Magha was only king for four years before his death. He was succeeded by Mansa Sulayman, who was his uncle. Unlike Mansa Musa, who was loved by his subjects, Mansa Sulayman was very unpopular as the people didn't like him. Although he was unpopular, he was very skillful in the act of leadership and was powerful. During the reign of Mansa Sulayman, Ibn Battuta, the Arab geographer, visited Mali between 1352 to 1353. So, there is much information available about the empire administration under the rule of Mansa Sulayman. Sulayman reigned from 1341 to 1360 and during his reign, audiences were held that permitted the citizens to come and present their complaints or disputes before the king. Some of these audiences were held in the royal court. This court was described as a "lofty pavilion" that had gilded arches on the side and long curtains by Ibn Battuta. The curtains were raised, and a flag hung outside the window, drums were beaten and trumpets blown before the king would sit. Other times, the audience was held at the base of a giant tree.

The king's throne was elevated with stairs, and a shade made of silk with a golden falcon placed on top of it was constructed over the throne. The falcon on top of the shade is similar to the one in the king's court. When the audience was held either in the king's court or under the tree, royal dignitaries and members of the king's cabinet would sit in the presence of the king. Outside, the honor guards numbering three hundred would line up according to their ranks, half of them armed with bows and arrows, and the other half with lances. Outside the palace, two rams were always present, which were believed to protect the king by warding off witchcraft. Also, there were always present two saddled horses that the king could decide to use at any time. Whenever the king appeared in public, he always wore a golden headdress and carried a bow and quiver, which was a symbol of power in Malian culture. Immediately after the king ascended the throne, his councilors, deputies, and all subordinate kings were summoned to come before the king before having their seats. All the king's subordinate kings had their own entourage made up of his personal honor guard armed with bows, quivers, and lances, and as they and their entourages walked towards the king, there were trumpeters and drummers marching in front of them.

Mansa Mari Jata II

Mansa Sulayman was succeeded after twenty-four years as king by his son Mansa Kanba in 1360. That same year, there was civil unrest because of the power tussle between Kanba and his cousin, Mansa Musa's son. This resulted in a civil war in the same year Mansa Kanba ascended the throne. Mansa Kanba died in 1373; he only ruled for nine months. He was succeeded by Mansa Mari Jata, who was the son of Mansa Magha and the grandson of the great Mansa Musa. Some historians believe Mari Jata was the same person invited by Kasa to overthrow her husband, Mansa Sulayman.

The succession struggle seed was sown during the reign of Mansa Musa. When Mansa Musa would go on a pilgrim, he would leave Magha in charge and when he died, Magha succeeded him; Mansa Musa's brother was grieved because he expected to be the next mansa being the most senior male in the family. Mansa Magha ruled only four years and he was then succeeded by Mansa Sulayman. Some schools of thought believe he was murdered by Sulayman. This, they say, could explain the reason the people disliked him and also the reason his wife would invite Jata to overthrow her husband.

Mansa Mari is known to be the most despotic king the Mali Empire ever had. He inflicted his people with much pain and suffering. He ruined the empire by destroying the principles of justice his predecessors had ruled by. Jata also depleted the empire's treasury. Among all his atrocities, the most infamous was the selling to Egyptian traders the empire's huge gold nugget at a meagre price. This gold nugget was the Mali Empire's most valuable national treasure. Mansa Jata died in 1373 after suffering from sleeping sickness.

Religion

The Mande society, which included the Mali Empire, had always believed in the spiritual realm. And this spiritual belief affected every area of their society, from their personal relations to carrying out trade. Traditionally, these people believed their relationship with inhabitants of the spirit world was affected by either their actions or inactions. In fact, several supernatural creatures had a specific name; now, they could all be referred to as jinn in Arabic, which was translated to genies. But as trade increased and caused the mixture of several cultures and religions, one of the religions that entered into West Africa through trade was Islam. Islam was introduced by Arab merchants who came to trade. There are two contrary records of when Islam became the official religion in the Mali Empire (that is, which of the kings first converted to Islam). One report is given by the Muslim chroniclers and travelers, Ibn Khaldin and Ibn Battuta, while the other comes from the oral tradition of the Malinke people.

While the former recorded that Sundiata, who was the first mansa, converted to Islam. The latter refutes the claim that Mansa Sundiata converted to Islam and abandoned their indigenous religion. It was, however, recognized that Islam was already in Mali even before the reign of the first monarch. It is recorded though that Mansa Uli, also known as Mansa Wali, Sundiata's son, went to Mecca as a pilgrim in the 1270s. This was followed by subsequent Mali kings as a tradition. The Malinke oral tradition is kept by the griots (special bards) from generation to generation.

Mansa Musa's reign is believed to be the peak of the Mali Empire's Islamization. He frequently pilgrimed to Mecca, and on his return, he brought back Islamic books, scholars, and even architects. These scholars taught in the Koranic schools as well as higher institutions he built. Although, the curriculum went further than just religious studies to include courses such as astronomy, history, medicine, and geography. These educational institutions rose to gain international recognition. The architects he brought designed buildings like the ones he saw in

Mecca, which included mosques. For example, the "great mosque," also known as Jingereber, was located in the cosmopolitan city of Timbuktu. The architects also designed great libraries containing thousands of manuscripts and books. Islam further spread into West Africa due to the influx of Muslim clerics into the region; these clerics were attracted to the region by the number of new converts. Also, citizens from Mali who converted to Islam traveled to Fez in Morocco to study, and many turned out to be great scholars, saints, and missionaries to neighboring territories. When indigenes of the region embraced Islam, the religion moved from being a foreign religion to one of Africa's religions.

Although Islam had gained ground in the entire region, the rural areas continued to practice their indigenous religion. This was recorded by Ibn Battuta in one of his visits to the Mali Empire in c. 1352. One of the reasons the indigenous religion continued to strive was that Islam was unpopular because it was only taught in Arabic and not in their local language. For this reason, Islam flourished only in the educated class and cities. Another reason Islam could not flourish in the rural areas was that it wasn't able to completely replace the Malian's ancient animist belief. This had an effect on the Islam that was practiced in Mali as many believed it to be adulterated and slightly differed from the one practiced in the Arab world.

Culture

The griots (storytellers) were custodians of the Malinke's legends. They were also responsible for orally transferring the empire's histories from generation to generation, even to this present day, and they mixed the stories with music. According to the Malian Empire's culture, there were special songs composed and sung only for some reputable citizens. This was the case for very talented and accompanied hunters and warriors. Sculptures made of solid pottery and usually measuring up to twenty inches in height were produced in areas like Djenne. These sculptures were sometimes made solid by adding iron rods to the interior. Other materials used for the production of sculpture include brass, wood, and stone. Paints were used to make decorations. Among the figures sculpted were warriors with beards riding on a horse. Other sculptures were crouching figures with faces turned upward; some of these sculptures were used for burial and ritual ceremonies, while others were used for decorating homes of wealthy citizens.

Decline

The Mali Empire flourished from the 13th century, and at the end of the 15th century, it began to decline. Just like every other empire before it, its progress and advancement attracted rivalry from neighboring kingdoms, and one of such kingdoms was the Songhai. The empire was also attacked in 1433 CE by the Tuaregs. Aside from the several attacks, the major reason for its disintegration was that it had no strict and defined laws for succession among members of the royal family. This led to succession conflicts between brothers and uncles and sometimes resulted in outright civil wars. Other attacks on the empire include the attack by the inhabitants of lands located to the south of Niger River, the Mossi people.

The Mali Empire was reduced to a shadow of its former great self. Due to the strong competition between European kingdoms for the control of West Africa, which would result in the control of the Saharan caravans, the one who controlled the caravans would control the most effective means of transporting goods (including slaves) to the Mediterranean. This competition and the presence of the Europeans reduced the authority the Mali Empire once had in the region. In 1468 CE, the

Songhai Empire, at its peak under the reign of King Sunni Ali, attacked and conquered the Mali Empire.

Chapter Eight

WHAT IS LEFT TODAY OF CLASSICAL AFRICAN KINGDOMS

Among the many kingdoms that existed in precolonial Africa, only a few of them are still standing today. In the whole of North Africa, for instance, none of the ancient kingdoms are still existing; in the Horn of Africa, only the Sultanate of Aussa and the Tooro Kingdom still stand. In West Africa, only the Asante Union still exists, while the Kuba Kingdom is the only empire that is still standing in Central Africa.

East Africa

Kingdom of Buganda

This empire is one from which the Ganda (Uganda) people emerge. It happens to be the largest empire in all of East Africa. The kingdom was called the name Muwaawa, before the coming of the 12th century.

Sultanate of Aussa

The Sultanate of Aussa was adopted into Ethiopia in 1945; however, the empire still had rulers appointed over them under the Ethiopian government. Therefore, the kingdom still had a certain level of independence between the 1950s and 1970s. Still today, the domain is under the Sultan's rule, the current Sultan being Hanfere Alimirah, who succeeded his father in 2011.

Tooro Kingdom

After it was established in 1830, the Kingdom of Tooro was incorporated into Bunyoro-Kitara in 1876. The people of the kingdom known as Batooro speak the same languages as the Bunyoro people; their cultures also have similar features.

West Africa

Asante Kingdom

The Ashanti Kingdom was established in 1695, and it is still standing today. It is a subnational empire that is protected by the constitution since being joined with the Republic of Ghana. Presently, it is being sustained through its dealing in cocoa, kola nuts, agriculture, and gold bars.

Central Africa

Kuba Kingdom

The Kuba Kingdom is a kingdom that is populated by people of the following tribes: Kete, Coofa, Mbeengi, and the Kasai Twa Pygmies. It is home to a total of nineteen separate tribes even to date. The ruler of the kingdom is referred to with the title *Nyim*.

Chapter 9

CONCLUSION

There is no doubt that kingdoms that existed in Africa before the coming of colonists were great empires having large and prosperous civilizations during their peak. They were mostly involved in the trade of items such as salt, ivory, textile materials and so on; some of them were able to mine gold from their lands.

Since the precolonial African empires were self-sufficient, they traded with European merchants for textiles and other commodities; and the Europeans who visited these kingdoms often marveled at how their governments were centralized and how well the rulers conducted their authority. A good number of these kingdoms conquered their neighbors in order to expand their territory and they became great enough to threaten European powers.

However, most of the precolonial kingdoms were affiliated in that they met their end (the kingdoms fell) due to a number of reasons, which include internal disputes among tribes, struggle for power among the rulers as well as priests, and the arrival of colonial masters.

Made in United States
Troutdale, OR
04/23/2024

19398303R00102